BAYARD T

THELATEGREATAPEDEBATE

Cincinnati, Ohio

Published by Standard Publishing, Cincinnati, Ohio

www.standardpub.com

Copyright © 2008 by Bayard Taylor

All rights reserved. No part of this book may be reproduced in any form, except for brief quotations in reviews, without the written permission of the publisher.

Also available: *The Late Great Ape Debate Discussion Guide*

Printed in the United States of America

Project editor: Robert Irvin

Cover and interior design: The DesignWorks Group

All Scripture quotations, unless otherwise indicated, are taken from the Holy Bible, NEW INTERNATIONAL VERSION®. NIV®. Copyright © 1973, 1978, 1984 by International Bible Society. Used by permission of Zondervan. All rights reserved.

Scriptures marked *KJV* are taken from the King James Version.

Scriptures marked *NKJV* are taken from the New King James Version. Copyright © 1982 by Thomas Nelson, Inc. Used by permission. All rights reserved.

Published in association with the Books & Such Literary Agency, Janet Kobobel Grant, 52 Mission Circle, Suite 122, PMB 170, Santa Rosa, CA 95409-5370, www.booksandsuch.biz.

ISBN 978-0-7847-2172-8

Library of Congress Cataloging-in-Publication Data

Taylor, Bayard.
   The late great ape debate / Bayard Taylor
      p. cm.
   Includes bibliographical references.
   ISBN 978-0-7847-2172-8 (perfect bound)
   1. Creation. 2. Creationism. 3. Evolution (Biology) 4. Religion and science. I. Title.
   BS651.T28 2008
   231.7'652—dc22

                                                                                2008001950

14 13 12 11 10 09 08 9 8 7 6 5 4 3 2 1

DEDICATION

To all who've ever been
troubled, confused, or made ill at ease
by the creation/evolution controversy;
and to anyone
who has ever put a fish,
a Darwin-fish,
or an anti-Darwin-fish sticker
on the rear bumper of his or her car.

CONTENTS

PLANET OF THE APES

A RUMBLE IN THE JUNGLE

DANCES WITH APES

NOTES

A DAY AT THE MUSEUM

On Memorial Day 2007, The Creation Museum—a $27 million, high-tech facility just outside Cincinnati—held its grand opening. By early evening 3,000 people were lined up to get inside. What was all the excitement about?

Inside, visitors found animatronic children in buckskin playing with baby tyrannosaurs; a re-created section of the Grand Canyon; and a special effects thrill ride through Bible history designed by the same man who also developed the Jaws and King Kong exhibits at the Universal Studios theme park in Florida.

The museum, built by Answers in Genesis (an organization founded by Ken Ham in 1994), is dedicated to the belief that God created the universe about 6,000 years ago and did so in six 24-hour days.

There was plenty of energy outside the museum as well. Protesters gathered with signs like "Do you deny gravity 2" and "Religion is the root cause of all terrorism."[1]

It's been more than eighty years since the Scopes "Monkey" Trial (which we'll look at shortly), and the creation/evolution controversy still generates a circus-like atmosphere and worldwide media attention. What is it about this debate that stokes such emotion and controversy? And how do we deal with it? That's partly what this book is about.

SCOPES "MONKEY" TRIAL: A watershed American legal case that tested a 1925 Tennessee law that made illegal the teaching of any theory that denied the concept of divine creation as taught in the Bible. It was tried in the summer of 1925 and received great publicity.

CREATION/EVOLUTION CONTROVERSY: A recurring debate across many circles—religious, philosophical, political—on the origins of man, life, the earth, and the universe itself. It has been greatly fueled by the studies and beliefs of nineteenth-century British scientist Charles Darwin.

EVOLUTION: In biology, the continuous genetic adaptation of living things to their environments through breeding, natural selection, and mutation. Charles Darwin is the modern originator of this theory. (Others had suggested similar ideas before Darwin, but Darwin was the first to produce what was to many a convincing case.)

• *Microevolution:* Incremental genetic changes that over time lead to new varieties within the same species (or very closely related species).

• *Macroevolution:* Incremental genetic changes that over great spans of time lead to whole new types (and species) of organisms.

Darwin's theory describes the mechanisms (genetic adaptation and natural selection) that drive both micro-evolution and macroevolution. *Note: Unless otherwise noted in this book, evolution will refer to Darwinism and subsequent refinements of Darwin's main theory.*

But that's not all. Another, larger issue lurks behind the creation/evolution debate.

THE NATURE OF NATURE

In high school American Literature class, many of us read at least portions of *Walden* by Henry David Thoreau. The nineteenth-century author isn't directly part of the Late Great Ape Debate. However, his attitudes toward God and nature are related, at least indirectly.

Something of a rabble-rouser, Thoreau liked to mix things up. And he sharply criticized civilization—and Christianity—in his famous book:

> *For most men, it appears to me, are in a strange uncertainty about [Nature[i]], whether it is of the devil or of God, and have somewhat hastily concluded that it is the chief end of man here to "glorify God and enjoy him forever."[2]*

Thoreau was really good at slams, and here he slams in a couple of different directions. First, he digs at comfortable people in polite, civilized society (most of whom considered themselves Christians) who were "strangely uncertain" about whether nature "is of the devil or of God." To them, God may have created nature, but they wanted to live as far away from it as possible. They saw nature as a raw, unpredictable, howling wilderness, a constant (almost demonic) threat that needed to be dominated and tamed.

Thoreau rejected that fearful attitude; he wanted to get back to nature to discover what it really was all about. He wanted to find out if nature—and life itself, through investigating nature—was ultimately "sublime" (awe-inspiring) or "mean." Nothing wrong with that!

ANOTHER, LARGER ISSUE LURKS BEHIND THE CREATION/ EVOLUTION DEBATE.

But to achieve this, Thoreau felt he needed to find a way around God-as-creator. So his second slam: "[People] have somewhat hastily concluded that

---

[i] Capitalizing the word *nature* when speaking about the natural world is common in some literary uses. For Thoreau, nature had nearly replaced God. So when he wrote about it, his practice was to capitalize the term, essentially giving nature the status of deity.

it is the chief end of man here to 'glorify God.'" This phrase, which nearly all of Thoreau's readers would have recognized at the time (but fewer and fewer people do today), comes from the then 200-year-old Westminster Catechism—a question-and-answer method for teaching basic Christian truth. (An assembly of church leaders produced it during the English Civil War of 1642-1651.) The first question of the Westminster teaching asked: "What is the chief end [purpose] of man?" Its answer: "to glorify God and enjoy him forever."

So what was Thoreau's point?

He believed worshiping God as creator and enjoying him is unnecessary and off the point! All people needed, he was arguing, was an intense, almost mystical experience of nature. Thoreau was attempting to give his audience a new "catechism" of sorts—just one that wasn't tied down to the Bible. But to build the foundations for his new religion, he had to tear down the old. So Thoreau the nature worshiper kicked the chair out from under what he saw as stodgy, inflexible Christian faith. It was, to him, now somewhat "hasty"—implying naive, simplistic, and thoughtless—to believe that our main purpose in life is to give honor to God and enjoy his presence in our lives now and forever.

> MAYBE I'M BEING TOO **SIMPLISTIC, NAIVE, THOUGHTLESS, AND HASTY,** BUT I THINK THOREAU MAY HAVE SOMEWHAT HASTILY CONCLUDED SOME THINGS HIMSELF.

Perhaps Thoreau was just trying to set up a weak argument so he could easily knock it down. I know plenty of Christians who absolutely love the great outdoors, who love nature and nature's God. Personally, I'm motivated by Thoreau's challenges to get outdoors and experience nature. However, I must differ with him on his nature worship riff. Maybe I'm being too simplistic, naive, thoughtless, and hasty, but I think Thoreau may have somewhat hastily concluded some things himself.

For example, Thoreau dismissed the overarching purpose of nature—which, ironically, *is* to glorify God. God intended nature to be a grand testimony to his power, creativity, and majesty. Nature's chief purpose is to point people to the one who's responsible for all this vast complexity and beauty (Psalm 19:1-4; Romans 1:20).

God also wants nature itself to enjoy *him*! God calls all of nature to party! "Let the rivers clap their hands, let the mountains sing together for joy" (Psalm 98:8). "The mountains and hills will burst into song before you, and all the trees of the field will clap their hands" (Isaiah 55:12).

If these things are so, how much more ought we humans take part! The Scriptures tell us that nature is leading the way for us! So that's also what this book is about. I want people to catch a greater appreciation for God's awesome works in nature *and* his mighty arm in salvation.

A NIGHT AT THE MUSEUM

What if you were tricked into taking a job as a night watchman for a haunted museum? What if all the museum displays came alive once the sun went down? And what if you didn't know the layout of the place and didn't know how to get out? Bummer, huh?

The creation/evolution debate is sort of like that: kind of spooky, and you don't know when the next exhibit is going to come off the wall and wallop you on the head. So here's a heads-up on the floor plan of the debate as presented in this book.

In Part I, "Planet of the Apes," we'll do a quick walk-through of the entire museum. We'll look at the Scopes Trial (chapter 1); introduce the agendas behind the issues (chapter 2); go over the five major approaches to creation and evolution (chapter 3); talk about ways to slice and dice those positions (chapter 4); and think about what it means to say that the Bible is God's Word (chapter 5).

> THE CREATION/EVOLUTION DEBATE IS SORT OF LIKE THAT: **KIND OF SPOOKY, AND YOU DON'T KNOW WHEN THE NEXT EXHIBIT IS GOING TO COME OFF THE WALL AND WALLOP YOU ON THE HEAD.**

In Part II, "A Rumble in the Jungle," we'll spend some extra time in each of the main halls, getting a little closer view of what the controversy is all about. We'll tell the story of how evolution got to be so popular (chapter 6); consider the "rules" for doing science and religion (chapter 7); and trace how one so-called Christian position surrenders to an anti-God worldview (chapter 8). Then we'll move on to a closer look at the four main views taken by Christians with varying beliefs in this debate:

Young Earth Creationism (chapter 9); Old Earth Creationism (chapter 10); Intelligent Design (chapter 11); and Theistic Evolution (chapter 12).

INHERIT THE WIND: The 1955 Broadway play that fictionalized the Scopes Trial. It was made into a blockbuster 1960 Hollywood movie, three TV remakes, and had a later reappearance on Broadway.

In Part III, "Dances with Apes," we'll go behind the scenes into the museum archives. We'll explore the propaganda of the play and movie *Inherit the Wind* (chapter 13); we'll look at the most important creation/evolution trials of recent decades (chapter 14); and I'll share my own creation/evolution journey, including what I taught my kids (chapter 15).

May this little tour start many future conversations!

Bayard Taylor
Ventura, California

PLANETOFTHEAPES

01 CULTOFTHEHAIRYAPE

There are 193 species of monkeys and apes, 192 of them are covered with hair.
The exception is a naked ape self-named Homo sapiens.
—DESMOND MORRIS, BRITISH ANTHROPOLOGIST (1928–)

Some call it Evolution,
And others call it God.
—WILLIAM HERBET CARRUTH, US POET (1859–1929)

In 1859, science got religion.

To be sure, it wasn't Christian religion. Nineteenth-century English biologist and educator T. H. Huxley—an ardent supporter of Charles Darwin—ruled that out when he said, "Evolution excludes creation and all other kinds of supernatural intervention."[3] It wasn't even a watered-down form of Christianity called deism, which accepts a creator but doesn't believe that he does much in the world.[4]

DEISM: The belief that a creator-God formed the world and set its physical laws in place, but takes no further part in its functioning.

CHARLES DARWIN: English biologist and naturalist (1809-1872) who originated the theory of evolution by natural selection. Earlier in life he believed in God before his work led to his apparent abandonment of faith.

Nevertheless, evolutionism became a new "religion," religiously held. Complete with its high priest and prophet (Darwin), its holy text (the just-published *On the Origin of Species*), its sacred places (the Galapagos Islands and the British Museum), its preachers (like Darwin and his "bulldog," Huxley), its new ethic (struggle for existence through natural selection and survival of the fittest), its holy grail (missing links, or the transitional fossils between species), and its mythic voyage over the seas (the trip of the HMS *Beagle*), this new religion—what we might call the cult of the hairy ape—captured imaginations on both sides of the Atlantic.

What was Darwinism's appeal? For one thing, what it was selling wasn't Christianity, a religion that to more than a few in the educated classes seemed tired and on its last legs.

For another, the cult of the hairy ape clothed itself in all the authority and excitement of discovery on the march, of science invincible, of triumphant reason. It had persuasive explanations for the incredible variations found in biology. It had potential to influence many fields of knowledge. And it made bold new assertions—not merely in man descending from the apes, but in the claims of tracing all of life back to tide pools and non-mammalian ancestors. As poet Langdon Smith whimsically put it:

> Let us drink anew to the time when you
> Were a Tadpole and I was a Fish.[5]

In short, the hairy ape cult supplied agnostics and atheists with something they never had before: a seemingly unbeatable, grand narrative for the origins of life, one that was based on the sure results of science. It didn't take long for evolutionism to trickle down from the universities and places of elite opinion to the public schools. And this brings us to the famous—or infamous, depending on your point of view—Scopes "Monkey" Trial of 1925.

MONKEY TRIAL OR KANGAROO COURT?

The Scopes trial was pure spectacle: part publicity stunt and part carnival; part camp meeting and part camp; part high theater and part politics; part inquisition and part serious trial. It was the first mass media event in American history: the details were rolled out before the breathless public through radio, newsreels in movie theaters, and in hundreds of newspapers across the country.

As a publicity stunt, the boosters for the city of Dayton, Tennessee, had arranged with the American Civil Liberties Union (ACLU) to bring fame to the city by staging a test of the recently enacted Tennessee law prohibiting the teaching of evolution in public high schools. John T. Scopes, a part-time football coach and teacher, volunteered to be a law-breaking guinea pig for the trial.[6]

THE AMERICAN CIVIL LIBERTIES UNION (ACLU): The ACLU is a massive legal and political organization (with more than 500,000 members as of the latter half of this decade) that focuses on litigation, lobbying, communication, and education. In 1925, it had been in existence for just five years.

As carnival and camp, the people of Dayton got behind the event in a big way. They put religious banners and signs up all over town that said things like "READ YOUR BIBLE"[7]; there were chimp posters and girls with monkey dolls; merchants sold souvenirs on the streets; and there was even a chimpanzee in a plaid suit and brown fedora sipping on Cokes at Robinson's drugstore.[8]

As a camp meeting, prayer meetings were held; preachers held forth in the open air; and songs, humorous and serious, were composed.[ii]

As high theater, two of the most well-known orators in the country were squaring off, and it was the first trial in American history to receive national media attention.

As politics, the always-emotional issue was church-state separation.

As inquisition, both evolution as an attack on Christian faith and the Christian faith itself were on trial.

The people who came to Dayton in July of 1925 would certainly get their money's worth.

And come they did.

> THE SCOPES TRIAL WAS PURE SPECTACLE: **PART PUBLICITY STUNT AND PART CARNIVAL; PART CAMP MEETING AND PART CAMP; PART HIGH THEATER AND PART POLITICS.**

I HEARD IT THROUGH THE APEVINE

The roadsides were lined with Model T cars, the courtroom jam-packed, the temperature hot and sultry. Let's journey back to the eighth and final day of the trial.

The previous day the lead defense lawyer, Clarence Darrow, had pulled a highly unorthodox legal move: he had called his opponent, the prosecuting attorney William Jennings Bryan, to the witness stand. Bryan agreed. During Darrow's questioning, Bryan said, "They are here to try revealed religion. I am here to defend it. . . . [Their] purpose is to cast ridicule on everybody who believes the Bible, and I am perfectly willing that the world should know that these gentlemen have no other purpose than ridiculing everyone who

---

[ii] Two of the humorous ones were "You Can't Make a Monkey Out of Me" and "Monkey Business Down in Tennessee."

believes in the Bible." Bryan also accused Darrow and other atheists and agnostics of "trying to force agnosticism on our colleges and on our schools, and the people of Tennessee will not permit it to be done."[9]

For his part, Darrow got in some pretty good shots of his own, directly attacking Bryan's beliefs, calling Bryan's faith "your fool religion" and saying, "We have the purpose of preventing bigots and ignoramuses from controlling the education of the United States, and you know it."[10]

The eighth day was full of surprises. Bryan was expecting to put Darrow on the stand, as Darrow had done to him the day before. But before that could happen . . .

Surprise #1: Even though it was highly relevant to the observers, the judge threw out the previous day's testimony as irrelevant to the legal issue at hand, which was whether Scopes had taught evolution.

Surprise #2: To get out of having to defend his own views on a witness stand and to speed up the appeals process, defense attorney Darrow elected not to go forward with the trial. Instead, he asked that the jury find his client *guilty*!

Surprise #3: The jury returned a quick guilty verdict and—presto!—the trial was over. Scopes was convicted and fined $100; creationism apparently had prevailed.

But in the court of public opinion, this legal "win" backfired into a public relations nightmare for both Dayton and Bible-believing Christians everywhere.

FROM MONKEYTOWN TO LAUGHINGSTOCK

How bad was it? So bad that much of conservative Christianity went culturally underground for half a century. This wasn't the kind of beating anyone would welcome, even fighting fundamentalists.

A few quotes from H. L. Mencken, a columnist for the *Baltimore Sun* whose daily reports were reprinted in the *Chattanooga News*, might help us catch the flavor. As you read, prepare yourself for an early twentieth-century journalistic style that—unlike today's reporters, who usually try to conceal them—instead showed off biases.

July 11. The selection of a jury to try Scopes, which went on all yesterday afternoon in the atmosphere of a blast furnace, showed to what extreme lengths the salvation of the local primates has been pushed. It was obvious after a few rounds that the jury would be unanimously hot for [in favor of a literal interpretation of] Genesis. The most that Mr. Darrow could hope for was to sneak in a few [members of the jury] bold enough to declare publicly that they would have to hear the evidence against Scopes before condemning him.[11]

Mencken didn't just question the potential fairness of the Dayton jury. He twirled his colorful pen to make Darrow into a giant among men and Bryan a menacing fool.

July 14. The net effect of Clarence Darrow's great speech yesterday seems to be precisely the same as if he had bawled it up a rainspout in the interior of Afghanistan. . . . During the whole time of its delivery the old mountebank[iii], Bryan, sat tight-lipped and unmoved. There is, of course, no reason why it should have shaken him. He has these hillbillies locked up in his pen and he knows it. . . . They understand his peculiar imbecilities. His nonsense is their ideal of sense. When he deluges them with his theologic bilge they rejoice like pilgrims disporting in the river Jordan . . . [12]

Notice how Mencken describes an evolutionist professor's reason and clarity against the seemingly irrational emotionalism of Bryan and the townspeople.

July 16. Then began one of the clearest, most succinct and withal most eloquent presentations of the case for the evolutionists that I have ever heard. The doctor [Maynard Metcalf of Johns Hopkins University] was never at a loss for a word, and his ideas flowed freely and smoothly. . . . what he got over before he finished was a superb counterblast to the fundamentalist [barrage]. . . . [Bryan, a three-time Democratic candidate for the US presidency] can never be the peasants' President, but there is still a chance to be the peasants' Pope. He leads a new crusade, his bald head glistening, his face streaming with sweat, his chest heaving beneath his rumpled alpaca coat. One somehow pities him, despite his so palpable imbecilities. It is a tragedy, indeed, to begin life as a hero and to end it as a buffoon. But let no one,

---

iii Merriam-Webster's Eleventh Edition defines this colorful word as "a person who sells quack medicines from a platform" or "a boastful unscrupulous pretender."

laughing at him, underestimate the magic that lies in his black, malignant eye, his frayed but still eloquent voice. He can shake and inflame these poor ignoramuses as no other man among us can shake and inflame them, and he is desperately eager to order the charge. In Tennessee he is drilling his army. The big battles, he believes, will be fought elsewhere.[13]

THOU SHALT NOT THINK[iv] [14]

The famous trial certainly entertained. But beneath all the playfulness and the circus atmosphere, the deepest convictions in people clashed. Mencken, among others, thought of those who believed the Bible literally as unenlightened and unthinking. His July 18 opinion piece read:

> BENEATH THE PLAYFULNESS AND THE CIRCUS ATMOSPHERE THE DEEPEST CONVICTIONS IN PEOPLE CLASHED.

Darrow has lost this case. It was lost long before he came to Dayton. But it seems to me that he has nevertheless performed a great public service by fighting it to a finish and in a perfectly serious way. Let no one mistake it for comedy, farcical though it may be in all its details. It serves notice on the country that Neanderthal man is organizing in these forlorn backwaters of the land, led by a fanatic, rid of sense and devoid of conscience. Tennessee, challenging him too timorously and too late, now sees its courts converted into camp meetings and its Bill of Rights made a [mockery] of by its sworn officers of the law. There are other States that had better look to their arsenals before the Hun is at their gates.[15]

The big Scopes "Monkey" Trial of 1925 was over.

Or was it?

We might call the Scopes Trial the O. J. Simpson trial of the 1920s. And much like the 1995 Simpson trial (the former football star was acquitted of two counts of murder), the Scopes trial served as a watershed cultural event,

---

[iv] A political cartoon of the time had a man representing William Jennings Bryan pointing a child's attention to a sign that read "THOU SHALT NOT THINK."

revealing conflicts and points of tension that still create a lot of heat even to this day. Some are obvious, some less so. Here are a few:

religion	vs. science (or, the proper place of science in Christian belief and teaching);
the Bible	vs. Darwinism;
God's design	vs. random mutation and natural selection;
meaning and purpose to life	vs. no meaning or purpose;
morality based on Scripture	vs. ethics based on human reason;
love your neighbor	vs. do whatever it takes to survive;
legitimate Bible interpretation	vs. making it say what you want to hear;
religious freedom	vs. separation of church and state;
the politics of the ACLU:	
appropriate	vs. inappropriate;
community standards	vs. civil liberties;
freedom of speech	vs. the control of speech;
conservative	vs. liberal;
small town	vs. big city (or, the perceptions of);
traditional	vs. modern (again, perceptions);
tolerance	vs. intolerance (did we mention perceptions?);
appropriate	vs. inappropriate definitions of science and religion;

the debate of what public school teachers should teach;
fear and distrust between Christians and secularists;
and, of course—
the ancestral relationship—if any—between humans and apes.

THE LATE GREAT APE DEBATE

Technically, Darwin didn't spark the human-ape debate. For a long time before him, people had speculated on the biological relationship between apes, chimpanzees, gorillas, gibbons, orangutans, monkeys, and humans, as well as what that relationship might imply. Darwin's theories simply added intellectual firepower to the speculation.

Thomas Henry Huxley (1825-1895) gets credit for fanning the flames of this debate into a blaze. Noting the biological similarities between gorillas, chimpanzees, and humans, he reasoned that since gorillas and chimpanzees came from Africa, so did humans, and the three likely had a common African ancestor. In the summer of 1860, the British Association for the Advancement of Science arranged for five distinguished experts to debate the subject. In a famous exchange, Samuel Wilberforce, the Bishop of Oxford and one of the learned experts opposing Huxley, asked his opponent whether it was on his father's or his mother's side of the family from which he traced his ape lineage. Huxley replied that given the choice between "a miserable ape" and a man of learning who would introduce ridicule in a serious scientific meeting, "I unhesitatingly affirm my preference for the ape."[16]

WAS HE ONE OF THOSE WILBERFORCES? Samuel Wilberforce was the third son of William Wilberforce, the famous English politician and abolitionist who fought a long battle to bring an end to the slave trade in the British Empire. (He was the hero of the 2007 movie *Amazing Grace*.) Samuel eventually became the bishop of the Anglican Church in Oxford. At the time of the debate, he was also Lord Bishop of Oxford, a member of the House of Lords, and a Fellow of the Royal Society, one of the oldest and most prestigious academic societies in Europe.

That little moment in science history is what this book considers the formal kickoff of the Late Great Ape Debate.

It is *late* because it has been going on "lately" in western history, since Darwin. It is *great* because it raises far-reaching questions for us and our society. As Mencken wrote, "Let no one mistake it for comedy, farcical though it may be in all its details." It is *ape* because it cuts to whether we see ourselves as made in the image of God or merely as cousins of apes. And it is a *debate* because people dispute this subject to death anyway, so we might as well find a way to discuss it, air our opinions, and voice our disagreements in such a way that we can live with each other.

In one sense, the Late Great Ape Debate won't ever die because it is part of the bigger stories we tell (or don't tell) about the meaning of life. During the trial Mencken scouted around for things in and around Dayton on which to report. He learned about an old-timer in the mountains who was supposed to know a lot about the Bible. When Mencken found the guy, he was amazed the old mountaineer could read the Bible in Hebrew and Greek. Mencken asked the old-timer to share his theory on the origins of life. The old-timer said, "Well, see yon hills? They know and they don't say. And I know, and I don't say."[17]

> IT IS A DEBATE BECAUSE PEOPLE DISPUTE THIS SUBJECT TO DEATH ANYWAY, SO **WE MIGHT AS WELL FIND A WAY TO DISCUSS IT, AIR OUR OPINIONS, AND VOICE OUR DISAGREEMENTS.**

That's the "don't tell" side. On the "tell" side, I hope this book can start people discussing the Late Great Ape Debate in a new way, a way that highlights the major controlling worldviews behind the debate, a way that respects what the various Christian responses are trying to accomplish, and in a way that better communicates the gospel of Jesus Christ in our culture.

02 VERYAPEANDVERYNICE

But man, proud man,
Drest in a little brief authority,
Most ignorant of what he's most assured,
His glassy essence, like an angry ape,
Plays such fantastic tricks before high heaven
As make the angels weep; who, with our spleens,
Would all themselves laugh mortal.
—WILLIAM SHAKESPEARE (1564-1616),
FROM *MEASURE FOR MEASURE*

Theater Patron: Hey, what's this show about, anyway?
Theater Patron: I don't know—they say it's some big gorilla.
Theater Patron: Oh . . . ain't we got enough of them in New York?
—FROM THE MOVIE *KING KONG* (1933)

If you just picked this book up out of curiosity, here's a courtesy preview of what it's *not* about:

- It's not about the ethical treatment of apes.
- It's not about whether apes can be trained to do sign language.
- It's not about whether we should send apes into space.

Rather, it's about looking at the ongoing creation/evolution debate in some new ways. I'm going to try to take you down a few different trails from the usual ones in this debate. I'm also going to ask you to think of this controversy through the lenses of worldviews and theology instead of just one view of right or wrong.

WORLDVIEW: The mental grid (ideals and beliefs) through which one filters his or her view of the world.

THEOLOGY: The study of religious faith, practice, and experience; the study of God and God's relation to the world.

Here's one thing I'm not going to do: bang you over the head with scientific facts and try to prove to you that there is only one rational way of looking at this problem.

TO GO APE OR NOT TO GO APE—THAT IS THE QUESTION

You've surely noticed that there's often an almost unbearable tension in how people feel about science and religion. This topic really gets people's juices flowing. In some places the debate's gotten so downright contentious and nasty that it's hard to take any position without somebody going off and calling you names.

How do people respond to this situation? Emotionally, you'll find both flight and fight responses. Some flinch at the mere mention of the concept and just want to clam up and run for cover. They hate mixing it up or getting others riled. Others revel in the conflict and get right up in your face. If they can bring

IN SOME PLACES THE DEBATE'S GOTTEN
SO DOWNRIGHT CONTENTIOUS AND NASTY
THAT **IT'S HARD TO TAKE ANY POSITION**
WITHOUT SOMEBODY GOING OFF AND
CALLING YOU NAMES.

insulting and abusive language into the debate, all the better!

Intellectually, you'll often hear people on TV or the radio, or maybe in something you read online, arguing strenuously for their positions against all others. In effect they're saying, "I'm right and you're wrong. And I'm going to show you backwards and forwards how pitiful your arguments are. Then if you still don't agree with me, I'm going to demonstrate up and down how dumb you are."

In the face of such intensity, I say, "Chill!" Let's all calm down a bit, step back, and take a deep breath. Let's try to get the big picture. Let's use a little empathy and try to look at what other people believe and why they believe that way. Let's all try to have a little civility. And let's try to help each other make more informed choices.

With that in mind, here are some things to think about.

First, there's more than one way to think about the relationship between creation and evolution. It's not just choosing for God and the Bible against any form of evolution, or choosing for science and reason against God and the Bible. Within Christian faith, you've got options.

Second, we're going to boil the options down into five basic types—but only four of them are viable options for believing Christians, as I will explain. We'll look squarely at the pros and the cons of each. You're going to find that each perspective has some positive things that are important to consider and values worthy to preserve. You're also going to find that each perspective has hardships that it alone must bear—real difficulties, not just fake ones. No option gets away without *someone* having a problem with it.

This goes against the common attitude that says, "If you just look at the facts and understand what I'm saying, you'll see there are no problems with my position at all." No perspective is without predicaments, perplexities, and paradoxes. Therefore, the best choice will *not* be the one position that effortlessly answers all questions with no troubles whatsoever. Rather, the best choice will be the position that makes you the least uncomfortable, the one you can live with despite its problems.

Owning up to the hard parts of your position is a more honest way of dealing with things than pretending that everything is just perfect. What I'm offering here isn't a perfectly soft couch to lie on, but it's not a bed of nails either.

Third, we're not going to get bogged down in overly technical scientific arguments. Sure, we'll need to talk some science, but as I said before, I'm not going to try to snow you with complex vocabulary and obscure facts. As someone who's not a scientist but who has studied science, I'm going to try to respect that field and yet keep things as simple and clear as possible. (If you want detailed, technical science, read more of the works cited in the Notes section at the back of this book.)

Fourth, I'm not going to try to paint anybody into a corner or bind your conscience to a particular point of view. I invite you to disagree with me! And I promise I won't body-slam you if you do. I'd much rather have you get angry and engaged than passively accept everything I say. I want you to wrestle with this stuff, to be challenged by it, and to always be thinking, "What's he saying that for?"

> **I INVITE YOU TO DISAGREE WITH ME!** AND I PROMISE I WON'T BODY-SLAM YOU IF YOU DO.

Fifth, we're going to dive into some fascinating stories. We've already briefly revisited the famous Scopes "Monkey" Trial. We'll also look at Galileo's heresy trial (1633), the fictional *Inherit the Wind* play (which later spawned the 1960 movie), and the recent efforts (2005) to keep Intelligent Design out of school science textbooks in Dover, Pennsylvania. Along the way we'll try to have some fun with chapter titles and subtitles. As an added bonus and at no extra charge, I'll share some of my story with you. At one time or another in my life, I've held each of the various creation/evolution positions that we're going to discuss.

ME TARZAN, YOU JANE

One day on the back lot of the movie *Tarzan the Ape Man*, Maureen O'Sullivan was struggling with a heavy suitcase. Johnny Weissmuller effortlessly lifted it up and slung it into her car, playfully quipping, "Me Tarzan, you Jane." The cast and crew who heard it thought it so funny and repeated it so many times that the phrase lives on to this day.[18]

Like Weissmuller's character, I may not be the most articulate guy around. However, I do hope to create a conversational space where people coming from completely different creation/evolution perspectives can meet together and discuss these things in a civilized way.

So here's something that's been bugging me for a long time. I couldn't quite put my finger on what it was exactly, but recently, after it came to me more clearly, the following diagram came to mind.

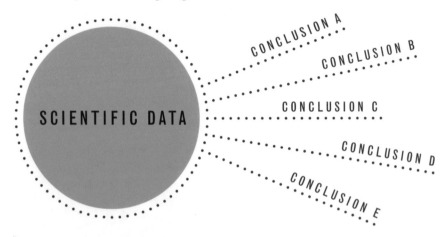

The basic issue is: How can reasonably intelligent people look at the same scientific "data" set (I'm using *data* in the loosest possible sense, as whatever people accept as facts) regarding evolution, yet come up with radically different conclusions? More specifically, why do some people take any evidence for evolution to mean that God must not exist and that science disproves the Bible—while at the same time others take the same evidence and conclude that science proves God's existence and the truth of the Bible?

Clearly, something's at work here other than the scientific data itself. For now, let me call that something *agendas*. More than all the clever and ingenious arguments on all sides, agendas accepted or chosen *before the science ever begins* predetermine the conclusions about God and the Bible. Agendas cause people to see selectively; they drive interpretations. Agendas are used to preserve the things people consider of the highest value. They cause people to shun things that they consider intolerable.

I want to understand how these agendas work.

MONKEY SEE, MONKEY DO

At this point we run right into one of the most interesting, and universal, facts of human experience: In many ways that we don't fully understand, we're shaped by the people and the culture around us.

This shaping carries with it all kinds of assumptions that go into effect before we ever start receiving or processing experiences. We don't generally think much about those assumptions, so when we find others who disagree with us (about creation, evolution, and other things too), we often respond with us vs. them thinking:

- *They must be frozen in some kind of prehistoric, backwoods way of thinking.*

- *They must be dishonest and are just saying those things for the money or power they hope to gain.*

- *They just don't have sufficient mental capacity; if they disagree with me, they're obviously a few bricks shy of a load.*

- *They're just plain evil.*

This assigning of villains and heroes—of deciding who's with us and who's against us—might make us feel superior, but it doesn't help us understand what's going on. It also ignores four critical debates stirring around underneath the surface of the big debate we're interested in. These four submerged debates are just as important, if not more so, than the Late Great Ape Debate itself. Let's introduce them.

1. The Debate over Worldviews

Your worldview is the mental grid you use to filter your experience of the world. It's also the framework for ordering and interpreting those experiences. Worldview defines your understanding of God, truth, meaning, and morals. In society, worldviews carry significant implications for education, economics, politics, and social policy. Most of the time, we don't think much about the worldview that we hold. But it's still there, guiding all of our thinking and action in the world. We can be guilty of passionately presuming that our way of looking at the world is the right way.

Everybody has a worldview, whether it includes or rejects religion.[v] Your worldview colors how you see things, events, facts, and stories. Your worldview has "rules" that only admit certain "facts" and how they may be read. This explains in part why people can look at the scientific data for or against evolution and interpret it in radically different ways.

One of the main worldview clashes in our culture is between the biblical worldview and the worldview of naturalism. The biblical worldview sees God as the creator of the universe (we are leaving open for now the question of how God chose to do it), holds that God acts freely in his universe, and believes that we can come into a relationship with God our creator through his Son, Jesus Christ, and through the Holy Spirit.

NATURALISM: A theory or worldview denying the supernatural realm and holding that scientific laws are adequate to account for the existence of all things.

Naturalism is a philosophy of life that categorically preempts God; a belief system that holds that scientific laws are adequate to account for all phenomena. This worldview asserts the cosmos, or nature, is all there is, all there ever was, and all there ever will be.[19] Naturalism is also known as materialism, physicalism, secular humanism, and atheism.

There's a big difference between being a *naturalist*—someone who loves and studies plants, birds, insects, and animals—and holding to the philosophy of naturalism. A naturalist could believe any worldview; naturalism assigns all ideas of God and religious doctrine to imaginary delusions.

2. The Debate over Science and Religion

A second debate is over the proper scope and limits of legitimate science and religion.

At this point I must digress for a moment to say that I dislike referring to the Christian faith as religion. To me, *religion* is a generic term, one that tends to

[v] For more on this, see *Blah, Blah, Blah: Making Sense of the World's Spiritual Chatter* (2006), by the author.

turn people off. It can smell of self-righteousness, even offensiveness. In many people's minds it implies rituals, structures, hierarchies, and formality that may or may not have anything to do with a dynamic relationship with God through Christ and the Holy Spirit. I'm not interested in Christian *religion*; I am very interested in the Christian *faith*. However, as a concession to common usage and as a convenient shorthand, occasionally you'll see me using the term *religion* in this way.

That said, how far should science press its claims into the spiritual and moral sphere? And how far should religion press its claims on science?

We'll come back to these questions in chapter 7. For now, let's put them on the back burner.

3. The Debate over Biblical Interpretation

A third debate is: Granted that people interpret the first chapters of the Bible in all kinds of ways, what's the best way, or most valid way, of reading these sacred texts?[vi]

People have a lot riding on their ways of interpreting the Bible. It's tied into their personal faith, their churches and other faith communities, and what they've been taught by people they respect who love the Lord. It's great when there's agreement; it's not so easy to disagree with your faith community or your spiritual leaders whose lifestyles have pointed you to Jesus.

Let's go a bit further with this. The illustration below shows an inner core ringed with expanding concentric circles, from what I'll call the white-hot core to virus alerts!

[vi] The Jewish Bible, originally written in Hebrew with a little Aramaic, is what Christians call the Old Testament. The New Testament, written about Jesus and concerning the community of believers springing from his ministry, reveals the fulfillment of Old Testament promises. It was originally written in Greek.

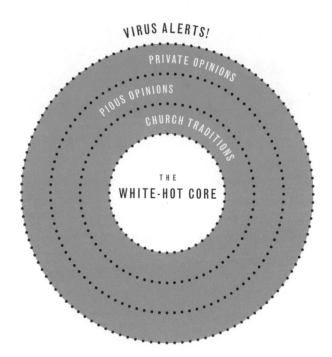

The white-hot core, as I'm defining it, holds that God has revealed himself to humanity. It holds to the biblical worldview and the gospel of salvation through Jesus Christ. It's wrapped up well in the Apostles' Creed, which first arose, many believe, around 150 AD in the middle of persecution, false teachings, and fierce competition with non-Christian religions. It has been affirmed by Christians East, West, North, and South throughout the ages. This core also would include the deeply rooted conviction and experience that Christians have of the Trinity: Father, Son, and Holy Spirit. White-hot core beliefs are first-order issues; everything else is second-order.

Next, church traditions are customs passed from generation to generation upon which some branches of Christian faith have been further built (rightly or wrongly). In this band we would find traditions such as those found in Eastern Orthodox churches, the Roman Catholic Church, and various forms of Protestant churches. Each group differs from the others in significant ways (such as how they understand church authority), but they adhere to many of the same tenets in the white-hot core. So church traditions can be further defined as *interpretations* of the core; they are not the part of the core itself.

The next wider circle represents pious opinions around which smaller groups of Christians gather. The reasons for defining pious opinion subgroups are less central, less clear, and even less authoritative than the inner two circles, but they can still be important for thinking through some of our spiritual questions. An example might be: Should the church emphasize holiness and separation from the world, or engagement, with the goal of transforming it?

Private opinions, the last circle, are speculations on matters about which the Bible says very little or nothing. It could be said of people with private opinions that they mainly want to "make up their own minds for themselves" and don't much care what anybody else thinks. While we could say that church traditions and pious opinions at least gravitate in the direction of the white-hot core, private opinions have little organic connection to the other inner circles. A lighthearted example might be: "All dogs go to Heaven."

Virus alerts are shown outside the circles because they represent false teachings. They are wolves in sheep's clothing, pretending to be Christian and at first glance looking innocent enough, but eventually launching vicious attacks against the white-hot core and the gospel of Jesus.

A big part of the creation/evolution controversy among Christians, then, is whether this or that interpretation of Genesis belongs in the central white-hot core and is therefore non-negotiable; or whether it should be pushed off to one of the outer circles; or whether it's a sneaky attack from outside the circles.

Christian teachers sometimes raise the stakes by placing their interpretations about creation and evolution and their interpretations of the relationship between science and religion in the central circle of the white-hot core. To suggest otherwise can make things dicey, since nobody likes it when his or her preferred viewpoint is bumped to a lower level of authority.

> THE WHITE-HOT CORE, AS I'M DEFINING IT, HOLDS THAT **GOD HAS REVEALED HIMSELF TO HUMANITY.** IT HOLDS TO THE BIBLICAL WORLDVIEW AND THE GOSPEL OF SALVATION THROUGH JESUS CHRIST.

On these kinds of questions, it's important to respect motives and accept good-faith differences of opinion. If people aren't trying to smuggle in virus alert false teachings, they might just be doing the best they can.

4. The Debate over What to Teach the Children

A fourth debate is what to teach children about evolution in public schools. And that debate quickly morphs into questions of intellectual freedom, community values, and the separation of church and state, each of which can easily bulldoze the first three debates into the ditch.

Adding to the confusion is the spottiness of science education in this country. Many high school and even college graduates don't know what science is about. They are unfamiliar with hypotheses, double-blind studies, and how a scientific theory is established or changes. As a result, some can't tell the difference between good science and wacky, pseudoscientific nonsense like astrology or Scientology or the "secrets" of the Great Pyramid.[20] But for that matter, many adults can't either, even ones carrying impressive educational resumes.

APE AND ESSENCE

I'd like to finish this chapter with two illustrations. The first is a report, widely covered in the media, that the first detailed comparison of the genetic blueprints of humans and chimpanzees find the two sets between 96 percent and 98.5 percent identical. Whether you agree with them or not, there are plenty of researchers who have called this an "elegant confirmation" of a shared genetic past and of Charles Darwin's theory of evolution.[21]

The second is the song by Kurt Cobain, former lead singer of Nirvana, called "Very Ape." In one line, Cobain says, "I'm very ape and very nice." I'm not going to pretend that I know what the words are about, since linguists, literary critics, and other experts in Nirvana lore have said that Cobain's lyrics can't be fully understood. But I'd like to give it a stab anyway. Maybe this is simplistic, but I think Cobain was trying to say that even though he may have descended from apes, or perhaps at times acted apelike, he still could be a really nice guy.

In these two illustrations you have, in a

> MAYBE THIS IS SIMPLISTIC, BUT I THINK COBAIN WAS TRYING TO SAY THAT EVEN THOUGH HE MAY HAVE DESCENDED FROM APES, OR PERHAPS AT TIMES ACTED APELIKE, HE STILL COULD BE A REALLY NICE GUY.

nutshell, what this book is about. What does it mean to be human? Are we "very ape"? (Merely animal? Cruel? Impulsive?) "Very nice"? (Noble? Compassionate? Spiritual?) Some combination? Something else?

Into that mix of ideas, one of the most essential things I can possibly say, one that some scientists get and others don't—and one I'm not sure Kurt Cobain ever heard before his 1994 death by suicide (and if he heard it, did it ever fully register in his soul?)—is this:

> So God created man in his own image . . . male and female he created them (Genesis 1:27).

The phrase "in his own image" is an extremely rich one, indicating characteristics such as the capacity for spiritual fellowship, the ability to create, and a shared sense of morality, justice, and beauty. God says males and females— from every culture and class, from every ethnic group—reflect the image of God in our own unique ways.

And that reality has profound implications. Two of those are:

- We can never reduce humans to mere biology or genetics.

- "Very ape and very nice" does not adequately answer the question "Who are we as human beings?"

Nothing I say in the following pages should be construed to take away from the fact that God has stamped his image indelibly on each and every one of us.

03 TAKIN' CARE OF (MONKEY) BUSINESS

Has Evolution Made a Monkey Out of You?
Ape to Man
The Evolution of Evolution
August 7th 9 pm/8 central
The History Channel
—*LOS ANGELES TIMES* FULL-PAGE AD (2005)

EVOLUTION WARS
The push to teach "Intelligent design"
raises a question: Does God have a place
in science class?
—*TIME MAGAZINE* COVER STORY (2005)

Kansas school board's evolution ruling angers science community: The Kansas State
School Board [votes] to remove the teaching of evolution from the state's science
curriculum.
—CNN WIRE SERVICE STORY (2005)

Eighty-plus years out from the Scopes Trial and the creation/evolution debate is still selling newspapers, national magazines, and even TV specials. What gives all this monkey business such enduring sizzle?[22]

We might have thought that this was old news, all out of proportion with events nearly 150 years old. But the issues raised in 1859 by Charles Darwin in *On the Origin of Species* are no less important to our generation than they were to his. How we think about Darwin's theory cuts to the heart of what we think about God, truth, morals, our place in the world, and the meaning of life.

Darwin himself was ready to provoke, ready to stir things up. Regarding the diversity of species he said, "God's will . . . had nothing to do with it." And with that neat little flick of his wrist, "science" had apparently overturned traditional, religious views of the universe. Humans, it would now seem, had arrived on the planet for no other reasons than "dumb luck and ruthless competition."[23]

With claims like these being thrown around, it's hard not to choose sides. In fact, we all have a dog in this fight. Neutrality is not possible.

And the stakes are not trivial. No one can avoid emotional investment in this controversy; it strikes so close to whom we believe ourselves to be.

From a sales perspective, the beauty of this product is, you don't have to create a need for it. It's already hard-wired to our deepest hopes and fears. We can't help but respond to it.

So how have people responded to the scientific data itself and to the massaging and spinning of that data? If it helps, think of this as a dramatic play, called *Scientific Data* (OK, the title could be more dramatic, but bear with me for now), with five major characters. Let the curtain rise!

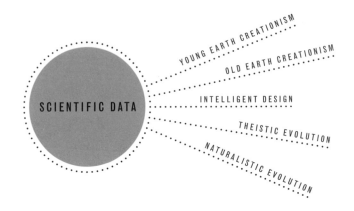

YOUNG EARTH CREATIONISM:
OH, GIVE ME A HOME WHERE THE DINOSAURS ROAM^{vii}

Enter, stage right: Young Earth Creationism (YEC). YEC holds to a straight-ahead literal interpretation of Genesis. According to this viewpoint, God created the heavens and the earth in six 24-hour days roughly 6,000 to 10,000 years ago, Noah's flood covered the entire earth, and humans and dinosaurs once coexisted. Some young earth creationists might be willing to stretch the creation out to, say, 25,000 years ago, suggesting that the word *day* in Genesis 1 (the Hebrew word is *yom*) could indicate an era, or epoch. But compared to the other approaches, young earthers believe that the earth came about very recently.

Regarding the vast diversity of life on the planet, young earthers teach *special creation*, the belief that God created all the different plants and creatures in that first week. Young earthers allow for microevolution, in which animals can change over time and develop traits *within* species that enhance their ability to survive, breed, and increase. But all young earthers reject Darwin's idea of macroevolution, in which species gradually change into new species. Darwinian evolution could not have happened, they say, because:

- The Bible says that God created the heavens and the earth in six days, and we should accept the plain meaning of the text.

- An array of dating methods in mainstream science is unreliable because the methods require vast amounts of time for evolution to work, time spans that contradict the Bible's genealogies, which can only be traced back a few thousand years.

- Most to all of the aged fossils were deposited in Noah's flood (Genesis 6-8), and the Grand Canyon was formed by it.[24]

- There is the testimony of Jesus. Regarding Noah's flood (which those in other camps may question as being a worldwide event), Jesus said in Luke 17:26, 27, "People were eating, drinking, marrying . . . Then the flood came and destroyed them all."

- Major gaps in the fossil record do not support the development of species from lower to more complex forms.

---

^{vii} The name comes from the Young Earth Creationism belief that dinosaurs and humans coexisted.

I'M LATE, I'M LATE FOR A VERY IMPORTANT DATE! Radiocarbon dating measures the age of bones and skin (organic materials) by the rate of decay of carbon-14 and is considered to be accurate up to about 50,000 years. For fossils and rocks (inorganic materials) other radioactive elements are used that are considered accurate up to millions or billions of years.

Scientists believe they have successfully correlated the carbon-14 method with other dating methods such as dendrochronology (comparative study of growth rings in trees and aged wood), magnetic fields captured in crystallizing rocks, ice core dating, and more.

Of course, young earthers reject these long time periods as contradictory to the Bible's chronology. They challenge key assumptions to the research, such as the relative stability of carbon-14 and the relative stability of the earth's magnetic field over vast periods of time. They would also suggest that the evidence points to an interpretation favorable to the Young Earth perspective.

(Sources: Edward T. Babinski, "Feedback for August 2002" on "Talk Origins Archive: Exploring the Creation-Evolution Controversy" at www.talkorigins.org/origins/feedback/aug02. html (accessed April 20, 2008); and "Doesn't Carbon-14 Dating Disprove the Bible?" by Mike Riddle on the Answers in Genesis Web site, www.answersingenesis.org/articles/nab/ does-c14-disprove-the-bible (accessed April 20, 2008).

• *The supposed missing links for common human and ape ancestry are mis-construed or have been faked, like the Piltdown man hoax. (We'll look at this more closely in chapter 12).*[25]

- *Randomness and the principle of entropy (the second law of thermodynamics) weaken the case against life emerging from nonlife, order arising out of disorder, or living creatures advancing into higher and higher levels of complexity.*

- *The Hebrew word translated* kind(s) *correlates to the term* species *(Genesis 1:21, 24, 25); therefore God created the living creatures so they could develop within their species, but not beyond them.*

- *The Bible says God specially created Adam out of the dirt of the ground and breathed into his nostrils the breath of life (Genesis 2:7). Therefore, humans do not have a common biological ancestry with bacteria, fungi, plants, fish, mollusks, reptiles, and mammals. If humans and all the other living creatures do have a common ancestor, God is a liar (because what God said in the Bible is not true), and the idea of humans uniquely created in God's image is fatally compromised.*

- *The Bible's start-to-finish narrative of the creation, fall, and redemption of mankind fits together better if one takes things the Bible's creation account literally.*

Albert Mohler, president of Southern Baptist Theological Seminary, a school that trains pastors for the largest Protestant denomination in the US, says:

> *Personally, I am a young-Earth creationist. I believe the Bible is adequately clear about how God created the world, and that its most natural reading points to a six-day creation that included not just the animal and plant species but the earth itself. . . . Evangelicals must absolutely affirm the special creation of Humans in God's image, with no physical evolution from any nonhuman species.*[26]

CONSISTENTLY LARGE PERCENTAGES OF AMERICANS POLLED SAY THAT GOD CREATED HUMANS "PRETTY MUCH IN THEIR PRESENT FORM WITHIN THE LAST 10,000 YEARS OR SO."

In our politically polarized culture, evangelicals often get a bad rap, so allow me to insert a definition that they would recognize and agree with: at the core of their beliefs is that the Bible is God's authoritative written Word. They affirm the historical fundamentals of Christian theology, and they want to bring the gospel of Jesus Christ to the whole world in word and deed.

Mohler acknowledges that some evangelicals think "it might have taken longer." But he asserts, "You cannot coherently affirm the Christian-truth claim and the dominant model of evolutionary theory at the same time."[27] His opinion is shared by many Christians; consistently large percentages of Americans polled say that God created humans "pretty much in their present form within the last 10,000 years or so."[28]

Important books in the Young Earth camp include John C. Whitcomb's *The Genesis Flood* (1961), Duane T. Gish's *Evolution: The Fossils Say No!* (1972), Henry M. Morris' *The Modern Creation Trilogy* (1996), and Ken Ham's *The Lie: Evolution* (1987).

Two well-known organizations that support the Young Earth Creationism view are The Institute for Creation Research ("revealing the truth of creation") and Answers in Genesis ("upholding the authority of the Bible from the very first verse"). The Institute for Creation Research (headquartered in Santee, California) sponsors speakers, conferences, and tours; produces books and other materials; has a graduate school; and runs the Museum of Creation and Earth History. Answers in Genesis (Hebron, Kentucky) sponsors magazines, provides online education, and curates the high-tech Creation Museum and Family Discovery Center, just outside Cincinnati, that I wrote about at the beginning of the book.

OLD EARTH CREATIONISM: STARLIGHT MONKEYS[viii]

Enter, stage middle-right: Old Earth Creationism (OEC). Old earthers take their name from the belief that our universe could be very, very old indeed. They bear no objections to the various dating methods used by mainstream science, accept mainstream disciplines of geology and astronomy, and might even say that the Bible came up with the idea of the Big Bang before scientists did.

They accept current theories that the earth is about 4.6 billion years old and the universe around 15 billion years old. They would say Big Bang

---

[viii] The name comes from the Old Earth belief that most starlight hitting the earth comes from objects many thousands of light-years away.

BIG BANG: The theory that the universe originated from an infinitely small point, or "singularity," in a gigantic explosion that kicked off the expansion of the universe between 12 billion and 20 billion years ago.

meshes quite well with the theological doctrine of creation *ex nihilo* (which is Latin for "out of nothing") and the statement in Hebrews 11:3:

> By faith we understand that the universe was formed at God's command, so that what is seen was not made out of what was visible.

Old earthers think that the earliest chapters of Genesis do not have to be read in a strictly literal way. For example, young earthers say the "days" of Genesis 1 were literal; Old Earth says the word *day* could be a literal day, an indefinite time ("in the day that the Lord God made the earth and the heavens," Genesis 2:4, *KJV*), or even eras or epochs ("With the Lord a day is like a thousand years, and a thousand years are like a day," 2 Peter 3:8). Another example: young earthers believe that that everything was perfect prior to man's sin; only after the fall of Adam and Eve in the Garden did death and disease come calling. Most Old Earth proponents would say that death existed before Adam and Eve sinned and that the fall is about how *spiritual* death infected humanity (see Romans 5:12-21).

Old earthers read in Genesis a faithful, sequential report of what happened in the beginning, through the perspective of the narrator. Hugh Ross, a preeminent voice on Old Earth Creationism in recent decades, displays the distinctive OEC approach when he compares Genesis to creation accounts from other cultures:

> Instead of another bizarre creation myth, here was a journal-like record of the earth's initial conditions—correctly described from the standpoint of astrophysics and geophysics—followed by a summary of the sequence of changes through which Earth came to be inhabited by living things and ultimately by humans. The account was simple, elegant, and scientifically accurate.[29]

According to this chronology, Day 1 is the creation of matter; Day 3 is the creation of life; and Day 6 is the special creation of humans, thus denying common descent of humans and apes.[30]

Most old earthers believe that God specially created Adam and Eve a few thousand years ago. On the other hand, many would not feel the need to try to press modern geology into the mold of Young Earth's worldwide flood.[31]

One portion of old earthers find themselves having no problems with many of the findings of modern physics and astronomy; they call their position progressive creationism.

> **PROGRESSIVE CREATIONISM:** The belief, within Old Earth Creationism, that God created life gradually, over a period of hundreds of millions of years.

They separate their position from other old earthers who subscribe to what has been called the gap theory. According to this theory (sometimes also called "ruin and restoration"):

- *In Genesis 1:1, God created matter and life millions or billions of years ago; a great expanse of time ("the gap") followed before we ever get to Genesis 1:2.[32]*

- *During the gap, multiple catastrophes caused massive extinctions that left behind lots of fossils (such as those of the dinosaurs), and in creation events God created new living organisms.*

- *Those holding to the gap version of Old Earth Creationism believe a huge flood wiped out most living things about 6,000 years ago.[33] After the flood, restoration began with the six days of Genesis 1.*

Like young earthers, old earthers accept microevolution but reject Darwinian macroevolution—for them, species were specially created by God apart from evolution. They deny that life can come from nonlife; they reject the idea of order coming from disorder; they dispute that the fossil record demonstrates evolution; and they counter assertions that DNA studies show

A PROMINENT VOICE FOR OLD EARTH: Hugh Ross is perhaps the best-known old earth creationist. He is an astronomer, physicist, author of *The Creator and the Cosmos* (1993) and *Creation and Time* (1994), and founder of the organization Reasons to Believe ("answering skeptics, encouraging believers"), based in Pasadena, California. His organization (www.reasons.org) has a stable of scholars who speak at conferences and churches, and Ross himself has a TV show on Trinity Broadcasting Network.[34]

the common descent of all life. For old earthers, people are created in God's image, and that idea excludes the possibility that people and apes have a common evolutionary ancestor.

Theologically, old earthers hold to a literal reading of the larger biblical narrative of creation-fall-redemption.

Other leading Old Earth Creationists are J. P. Moreland of Biola University, Gleason Archer of Trinity Evangelical Divinity School, and Walter Kaiser, president of Gordon-Conwell Theological Seminary.[35]

INTELLIGENT DESIGN: MONKEY WRENCHING[ix]

Enter up the center aisle: Intelligent Design (ID). The Intelligent Design movement is a restatement, in modern terminology, of a very old argument for God, the teleological argument—which means argument from design or purpose.

Psalm 19 uses a form of this argument as it begins, "The heavens declare the glory of God; and the firmament shows His handiwork" (Psalm 19:1, *NKJV*). Similarly, the apostle Paul uses a form of this argument in Romans 1:18-20. Verse 20 says, in part, "Since the creation of the world His invisible attributes are clearly seen, being understood by the things that are made" (*NKJV*).

In Christian history, some form of Intelligent Design has often cropped

---

[ix] The name comes from the Intelligent Design aim of tossing a "monkey wrench" into the finely tuned machine of philosophical naturalism.

up in philosophical theology. In the fourth century, Augustine used it in *The City of God*.[36] In the Middle Ages, Thomas Aquinas (1225-1274) employed it as his fifth argument for the existence of God.[37] And at the start of the nineteenth century, William Paley took the best of biological science available at the time and argued for God's existence in what would be his last book, *Natural Theology: or, Evidences of the Existence and Attributes of the Deity* (1802).[38] Paley's

> THE ARGUMENT FOR GOD FROM DESIGN WILL ALWAYS HAVE A POWERFUL, PERSUASIVE FORCE.

book was required reading for all Cambridge undergraduates—including Charles Darwin—for nearly fifty years after Paley's death.[39] Here's a sample of Paley's famous watchmaker argument:

> *Imagine yourself walking on a beach. If you stub your toe on a stone, you'll likely imagine that it happened there by purely natural processes. However, if you come across a watch, you'll likely realize that the watch, different from the stone, could not have occurred by accident, but was a mechanical device carefully designed to keep time. If we turn our gaze toward Nature and observe aspects of biology such as the eye, which is much more complex than a watch, we'll understand that an Intelligence (who is God) must be behind such marvels.[40]*

The argument for God from design will always have a powerful, persuasive force.

The contemporary Intelligent Design movement is defined by the phrase "irreducible complexity in biological systems." Michael J. Behe, a leading

> IRREDUCIBLE COMPLEXITY: The argument for a highly intelligent designer of biological systems (such as the human eye) that says those systems are too complex to have evolved from simpler, "less complete" predecessors.

proponent of this view and author of *Darwin's Black Box: The Biochemical Challenge to Evolution* (1996), likes to use the metaphor of the mousetrap. All the parts of the trap must be assembled in order for the thing to catch mice; if any one part is missing or improperly assembled, the gadget is useless.

Similarly, the human eye, the clotting of blood, and bacterial flagellum (the molecular motor and tail that enable bacterial cells to move) all exhibit irreducible complexity. ID says these incredibly complex biological systems could not have occurred gradually, that they must have happened all at once. Therefore, ID proponents point to an intelligent designer.

Intelligent Design followers prefer to present their viewpoint more as science and less as philosophy or theology. Here's how Behe, a Roman Catholic, professor at Lehigh University, and Senior Fellow of the Discovery Institute[41] put it in an interview for a *Time Magazine* cover story:

> We were taught in parochial school that Darwin's theory was the best guess at how God could have made life. I'm still not against Darwinian evolution on theological grounds. I'm against it on scientific grounds. I think God could have made life using apparently random mutation and natural selection. But my reading of the scientific evidence is that he did not do it that way, that there was a more active guiding.[42]

IF OLD EARTH CREATIONISM'S "BIBLICAL LITERALISM" TAKES A STEP AWAY FROM YOUNG EARTH CREATIONISM'S "STRICT BIBLICAL LITERALISM," **INTELLIGENT DESIGN TAKES A FEW STEPS MORE.**

To its advocates, Intelligent Design is a wedge that pries apart the worldview of naturalism from the practice of science.[43] The hope is that Intelligent Design can scientifically demonstrate the existence of God, challenge the deficiencies within Darwinism, and unmask naturalism as an anti-God worldview.

If Old Earth Creationism's "biblical literalism" takes a step away from Young Earth Creationism's "strict biblical literalism," Intelligent Design takes a few steps more. Like Old Earth Creationism, Intelligent Design is comfortable with the Big Bang and a universe of 15 billion to 20 billion years old. Unlike Young Earth and Old Earth, many Intelligent Design proponents would be comfortable

NO INTELLIGENCE ALLOWED: If you want to see an impassioned presentation of the Intelligent Design perspective (at least "impassioned" in what could be derived from the trailers and pre-release advertising), view the movie *Expelled: No Intelligence Allowed* (www.expelledthemovie.com). It stars Ben Stein and released in April 2008. The premise of the film is that "Big Science" silences the voices of those in the scientific community who believe the evidence points toward an intelligent designer.

The idea is to get viewers to question the authority of Big Science and Darwinism, both of which have been guilty of excluding God from the big picture.

allowing the Genesis 1 creation accounts to speak more poetically and less literally.

Intelligent Design's reasons for rejecting Darwin flow with the Young Earth and Old Earth assertions that macroevolution is only a theory; with the assertions that transitional fossils can't be found; and with the second law of thermodynamics ruling out increasing complexity in a closed system. Plus, all three say you can't fit evolution into the creation-fall-redemption narrative of Scripture.

Other pioneers of the Intelligent Design movement are University of California-Berkeley law professor Phillip Johnson, author of *Darwin on Trial* (1991), *Defeating Darwinism by Opening Minds* (1997), and *The Wedge of Truth* (2002); and William Dembski, research professor of philosophy and author of *Intelligent Design* (2002), *The Design Revolution* (2004), and *The Design Inference* (2006).

Two significant institutions that promote Intelligent Design worldwide are The Discovery Institute's Center for the Renewal of Science and Culture in Seattle, Washington, and Probe Ministries in Richardson, Texas.[44]

THEISTIC EVOLUTION:
CHIMPS, AHOY![x]

Enter stage middle-left: Theistic Evolution (TE). I'm not particularly thrilled about this name because left undefined theistic could refer to Baal, the storm-god of the ancient Canaanites; Molech, the child-eater of the biblical Ammonites; the unfeeling "first cause" and "unmoved mover" of the philosophers; the insincere, philandering Zeus of the Greeks; the Allah of Osama bin Ladin; there-are-many-gods polytheism; pantheism (in which everything is viewed as god); or even make-yourself-a-god of the New Age spiritualities. All this creates a confusing disharmony of voices that detracts from the beauty and uniqueness of the God of the Bible.

Unfortunately, I haven't been able to find a better name, and the term is commonly used. So in this book, when I use Theistic Evolution I'm referring to an evolution that involves not just any god or gods but the one true God, creator of the universe, who first revealed himself as Lord God (*Yahweh Adonai*) to the Jewish people and to Christians as God the Father, God the Son, and God the Holy Spirit (the Trinity).

Theistic Evolution is the belief that God created the universe in such a way that macroevolution happened. As Howard Van Till, a proponent of this view and physics and astronomy professor at Calvin College, says, creation was fully and "optimally equipped"[45] with all the potential needed to yield the richness, diversity, and complexity of life-forms and life-systems that we see today.

Theistic Evolution is not new. When Darwin's theory first came out, it caused tremendous controversy. Some saw it as a great threat. Others incorporated evolution into their theology. Still others took a wait-and-see attitude.[46]

Early on, Catholics divided along similar lines. After a century and a half of hashing things out, Theistic Evolution has won some measure of acceptance. In his 1996 message to the Pontifical Academy of Sciences, titled "On Evolution," Pope John Paul II said:

---

[x] The name comes from the Theistic Evolution belief that humans and chimpanzees genetically share an ancient common ancestor.

Today, more than a half-century after the appearance of [two earlier papal documents, one of which left some room for the possibility of Darwinian evolution], some new findings lead us toward the recognition of evolution as more than an hypothesis. In fact it is remarkable that this theory has had progressively greater influence on the spirit of researchers, following a series of discoveries in different scholarly disciplines. The convergence in the results of these independent studies—which was neither planned nor sought—constitutes in itself a significant argument in favor of the theory.[47]

"More than an hypothesis" was John Paul II's carefully worded way of saying that so long as God's providence was understood to be over evolution, evolution itself did not contradict Christian teachings. He was saying that it's possible to believe in the truth of the meaning of Genesis, the dignity and value of human beings created in the image of God, and in mainstream science, all at the same time. You don't have to make an either/or choice between evolution and the Bible.

Theistic Evolution proponents would say that Genesis 1 tells the story of our origins in a way that communicated perfectly well to its original audience, people who lived in a society without the science of today, about 3,500 years ago. They would argue that the Genesis 1 account focuses on the *who* of creation—not the *what* or the *how*, not the science or chronology of

'NO CONFLICT IN GOD AND . . . SCIENCE': Francis Collins, an evangelical Christian and the leader of the Human Genome Project (the successful ten-year attempt, accomplished in 2004, to map the genetic structure of DNA codes for human beings) is a theistic evolutionist. He says:

"I see no conflict in what the Bible tells me about God and what science tells me about nature. Like St. Augustine in AD 400, I do not find the wording of Genesis 1 and 2 to suggest a scientific textbook but a powerful and poetic description of God's intentions in creating the universe. The mechanism of creation is left unspecified."[48]

creation—and that the primary message is that God wants us to know he is the sovereign Lord over all of creation and superior to any other gods or goddesses that people mistakenly worship.

Other theistic evolutionists include Theodosius Dobzhansky (1900-1975), a pioneer in synthesizing evolutionary biology with genetics, and an Orthodox Christian; Kenneth R. Miller, a Roman Catholic, professor of microbiology at Brown University, and author of *Finding Darwin's God* (1999);[49] Darrell Falk, biology professor at Point Loma Nazarene University and author of *Coming to Peace with Science* (2004); and John Polkinghorne, an Anglican priest, practicing scientist, and author of many books, including *Science and Creation: Searching for Understanding.*

NATURALISTIC EVOLUTION: CLAN OF THE ANGRY MONKEY[xi]

And finally the spotlight turns to Naturalistic Evolution (NE), evolution that arises out of the philosophical-religious worldview of naturalism. Some have called this viewpoint evolutionism or scientism. I don't use these terms because I find them vague and confusing.

The Naturalistic Evolution lowdown on origins is that we are here as a result of nothing other than time, chance, and matter; life is just a cosmic accident; and when you get right down to it, our search for ultimate reason or meaning in life is a cosmic joke. The world is without design or purpose. Values become mere opinions or social conventions, untethered from any real concepts of right and wrong.

> TO BE SURE, **BAD BELIEFS** ABOUT GOD HAVE LED TO PLENTY OF MISERY.

Naturalistic evolutionists often seem to be mad at God (even though they don't believe he exists!), as if God, or belief in God, is the root cause of misery in the world. To be sure, bad beliefs about God have led to plenty of misery. But if life is all about survival of the fittest and nature that is "red with tooth and claw,"[50] why should a nonexistent God get so much blame?

[xi] The name refers to the irony that Naturalistic Evolution disbelief in God is so often accompanied by anger at God.

Worldviews are a lot like religions: every worldview wants to convince the world that it alone is true. With his many anti-God books, atheist and prolific author Richard Dawkins (*The Blind Watchmaker, The Selfish Gene, The God Delusion*) exhibits a fervent, missionary zeal. It's clear the British scientist's goal is to convert as many as possible to his worldview. In *The Blind Watchmaker* he writes:

> I want to persuade the reader, not just that the Darwinian world-view happens to be true, but that it is the only known theory that could, in principle, solve the mystery of our existence.[51]

As Dawkins puts it in another of his books, *River Out of Eden*:

> "The universe that we observe has precisely the properties we should expect if there is, at bottom, no design, no purpose, no evil and no good, nothing but blind, pitiless indifference."[52]

Whoa! Pretty depressing, huh?

Another expression of the religious aspect of this worldview is found in the work of E. O. Wilson (1929–), a Harvard professor, one of the most eminent evolutionary biologists of the last century, and the father of sociobiology (studying ethics as biology). Wilson claims that Darwin is hands down "the most important man who's ever lived" because he was the first human being "to see things as they really are." Pressed in a TV interview with Charlie Rose—"More important than Jesus, or Buddha?" Rose asked—Wilson affirmed his view.[53]

A ripe illustration is the National Association of Biology Teachers' 1995 Statement on Evolution:

> The diversity of life on earth is the outcome of evolution: an unsupervised, impersonal, unpredictable and natural process of temporal descent with genetic modification that is affected by natural selection, chance, historical contingencies and changing environments.[54] (Emphasis added.)

Notice the absolute nature of the words *unsupervised* and *impersonal*. Harsh, strongly expressed comments like these are widespread in the literature of this belief, starting with Charles Darwin, the grandfather of the movement,

DAWKINS CALLS HIMSELF "A RELIGIOUS NON-BELIEVER" AND SAYS, **"WHAT I SEE IN NATURE IS A MAGNIFICENT STRUCTURE THAT WE CAN COMPREHEND ONLY IMPERFECTLY,** AND THAT MUST FILL A THINKING PERSON WITH A FEELING OF HUMILITY."

and continuing down to Stephen Jay Gould's *The Structure of Evolutionary Theory* (2002), Dean Hamer's *The God Gene* (2004), and many others.

At its core, Naturalistic Evolutionism is reductionistic; it forces all of reality into a single cookie-cutter, that of materialism. In this worldview, appeals to "God" can never be anything more than vain wishful thinking, fearful responses to death, flights of fantasy, or cynical attempts to control others.

And yet, naturalistic evolutionists are human beings created in the image of God; therefore, their flamboyant denials of God cannot be regarded as their final word on the subject. People can change, and often do start thinking about eternal things as they get older. At the end of his life, from what I have read of his later writings, Gould had eased off his caustic attacks and left the door open a crack for God.

Dawkins himself, although he rejects any god along the lines of those found in monotheistic (single-god) religions, calls himself "a religious non-believer" and says, "What I see in Nature is a magnificent structure that we can comprehend only imperfectly, and that must fill a thinking person with a feeling of humility." He talks about "a pantheistic reverence [for nature] which many of us [scientists] share."[55] Wilson says in the first chapter of his book *Consilience* that it is only natural for people to reason backward from effects to causes to the "first cause," and that naturalism cannot refute the idea of God as creator. Furthermore, Wilson candidly opens his heart by sharing his longing to find grace, which led him to be "born again," baptized at fourteen:

> The still faithful might say I never truly knew grace, never had it; but they would be wrong. The truth is that I found it and abandoned it. . . . I was

enchanted with science as a means of explaining the physical world, which increasingly seemed to me to be the complete world. In essence, I still longed for grace, but rooted solidly on Earth.[56]

Here we find nature doing the job God intended it to do: to elicit from us who are created in God's image an indescribable sense of beauty, magnificence, and humility before something much greater than ourselves. Even dyed-in-the-wool atheists, it seems, are struck with wonder at creation. Every one of us, in our deepest heart, whether it agrees with our professed worldview or not, whether we admit it or not, says: "When I consider your heavens, the work of your fingers, the moon and the stars, which you have set in place, what is man that you are mindful of him, the son of man that you care for him?" (Psalm 8:3, 4)

It's not such a big jump from wonder to God.

04 TROLLINGWITHTROGLODYTES

What I am saying to you, is that you are the kind of club-toting, raw-meat-eating, Me-Tarzan-You-Jane-ing big bald bubblehead that can only count to ten if he's barefoot or wearing sandals.

—SANKA COFFIE IN THE MOVIE *COOL RUNNINGS* (1993)

Ever since primitive cave-dwellers, or troglodytes (which is one of my favorite words, by the way), began exploring their environment, we can imagine a fascinating scenario. Stand-up comics among them would observe that there are two kinds of people in the world: those who divide the world into two categories, and those who don't.

Kind of like Sanka Coffie in *Cool Runnings*. Some people are club-toting, raw-meat eating, Me-Tarzan-You-Jane-ing, big, bald bubbleheads who can only count to ten if they're barefoot or wearing sandals. And some aren't.

People tend to see things in different ways.

Here, we're going to take that either/or principle and play with it a little in breaking down the ways people look at the creation/evolution debate.

MEN IN MONKEY SUITS

For example, if we divide things up based on the biblical worldview versus the naturalistic worldview, then young earthers, old earthers, Intelligent Design proponents, and theistic evolutionists all see God's hand in creation. In spite of their disagreements about the *how* and the *when*, they're all creationists because their observations about life lead them to belief in a creator-God and the Bible as God's Word.[57] When they see a group of businessmen, they see more than men in cloth "monkey suits"—they see people created in God's image.

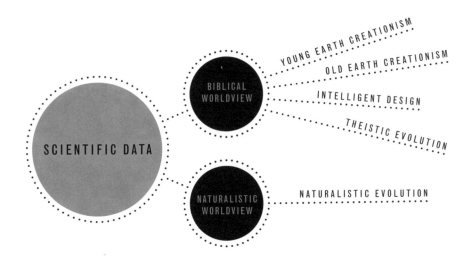

ON THE OTHER HAND, THE WORLDVIEW OF NATURALISM VIEWS THOSE SAME BUSINESSMEN AS **EVOLUTIONARILY ADVANCED AND RELATIVELY HAIRLESS MONKEYS.**

On the other hand, the worldview of naturalism, having dispensed with God and treating the spiritual side of humanity as mere chemical reactions in the body, views those same businessmen as evolutionarily advanced and relatively hairless monkeys.

THAT SIMIAN-I-AM, THAT SIMIAN-I-AM, I DO NOT LIKE THAT SIMIAN-I-AM

If we divide things according to how people emotionally react to evolution, a different pattern emerges.

Young earth and old earth creationists and most people in the Intelligent Design movement have a stomach-churning revulsion at the proposition that gorillas, orangutans, and gibbons might be our biological cousins. On the other hand, theistic evolutionists, along with atheistic and agnostic evolutionists, accept a biological connection in the order of primates. Theistic evolutionists still believe the anti-macroevolution folks are their brothers and sisters in Christ, but they think their brothers and sisters are wrong on how to put together science and faith.

ATHEISM: The belief that there is no God, or gods.

AGNOSTICISM: The belief that the human mind cannot know whether there is a God or an ultimate cause behind life and the universe.

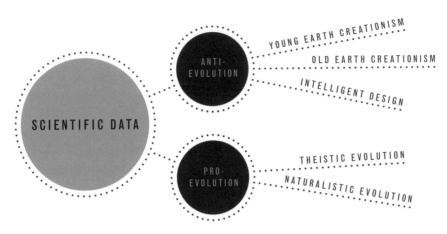

DON'T MAKE A MONKEY OUT OF ME

Young Earth and Old Earth Creationism, also seeking to preserve the idea that humans are created in God's image, don't want to be talked into believing anything that would contradict God's Word. These two approaches put a premium on believing the Bible by interpreting the creation accounts of Genesis 1 literally. According to this view, Intelligent Design is compromised because it takes too many things too metaphorically; Theistic Evolution is severely compromised because it plays too fast and loose with Genesis, turning the book into some kind of myth; and Naturalistic Evolution, naturally, is totally compromised because it rejects the Bible altogether.

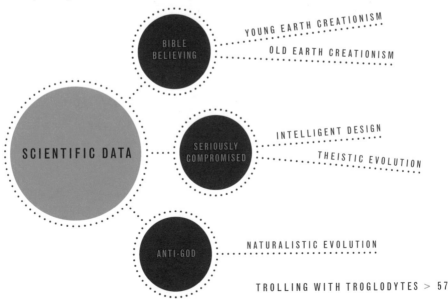

HANGING IN THE BALANCE

Another division would be according to Intelligent Design's desire to define the right balance between authoritative Scripture and the findings of science. Some ID proponents might find fault with young earthers *and* old earthers for not taking the historical and cultural context of the Bible seriously enough and for not taking science seriously enough. They would take theistic evolutionists to task for their interpretations of science and the Bible. And they would give naturalistic evolutionists a hard time for blindfolding themselves to the clear signs of God's intelligent design of nature. They would hope that their scientific arguments for Intelligent Design would open minds to consider the possibilities for belief in God.

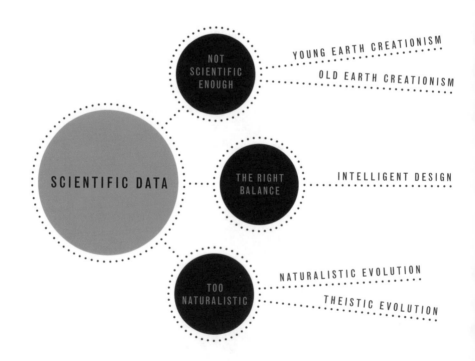

As a matter of record, just such a thing has happened in recent years for a fellow named Anthony Flew. Mr. Flew grew up the son of a Methodist minister. When in Oxford he got to know the famed twentieth-century author C. S. Lewis, a Christian. However, over his long career Flew carved out a place for himself as one of the most visible and vocal British non-believers in God.

Over the past several years, members of a group of Christian academics who believe in the power of the Intelligent Design argument have befriended Flew and invited him into a respectful dialogue. As a result, one of the world's once-leading atheists now says he is convinced, based upon the force of Intelligent Design as a scientific argument, that "a super-intelligence is the only good explanation for the origin of life and the complexity of nature."[58]

In 2004 Flew considered himself a deist, like Thomas Jefferson, whose God pretty much left people to work out their own affairs. Flew said, "I'm thinking of a God very different from the God of the Christians and far and away from the God of Islam, because both are depicted as omnipotent Oriental despots, cosmic Saddam Husseins."[59] And despite this flawed belief of God (when placed against how the Bible portrays him), more recently Flew has been growing his faith in other ways. He has been impressed by the work of John and Charles Wesley, ministers and theologians whose influence continues to uplift society two centuries after their deaths.[60]

THE WHO BEHIND "FROM GOO TO YOU"

Let's move on and look at things from the perspective of the theistic evolutionists who are working scientists, who publish scientific papers that are reviewed by peers, and who are working to expand the scientific knowledge base. They don't see the young earthers, old earthers, and Intelligent Design followers as doing real science. Rather, they find the attempts, by each of those three camps, to make sure there is science in their interpretations of Scripture as counterproductive to the whole scientific enterprise. From the theistic evolutionist standpoint, even if life started in a primordial soup of chemicals (the "goo"), science can't ultimately exclude God.

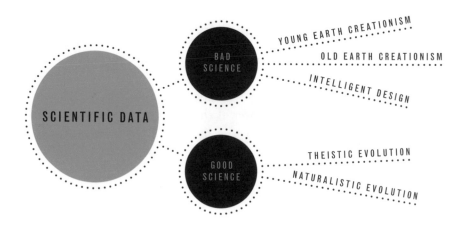

KNUCKLE-DRAGGERS OF THE WORLD: UNITE!

From the perspective of Naturalistic Evolution, we are knuckle-draggers who evolved into an upright stance, God had nothing to do with it, and anybody who disagrees is just plain knuckleheaded. Naturalistic evolutionists generally look with disdain and pity at those who still believe what they see as the fables and fairy tales of the biblical worldview.

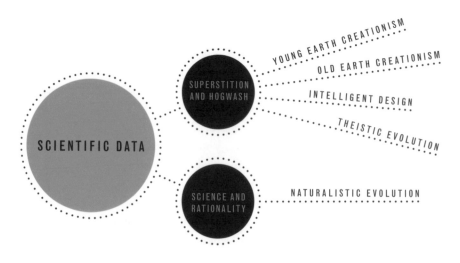

ON THE CAMPAIGN TRAIL: A SAVVY ANSWER

In the June 2007 Republican presidential primary debate, one of the moderators asked the candidates a poison-pill question: "Do you believe in evolution?" The question was designed to make the candidates squirm: If they said yes, they might well alienate their Christian political base. If they said no, it might well make them look foolish in the eyes of educated elites.

Mike Huckabee took the question head on and made it into a Martin Luther "Here I stand" moment. First, he denied Darwinian evolution and then defended his position by (a) defining evolution as believing that life and everything else came about by pure chance, apart from any involvement or working of an intelligent creator; and (b) explaining that he didn't know whether the earth was created 6,000 years ago or 6 billion years ago, but that, either way, God should get the credit.

While not everyone would agree with Huckabee, he did put his finger on a root worldview issue: the prejudice evident in some circles that belief in science necessarily excludes belief in God. (Note: This item is not intended as a political endorsement of any kind!)

The YouTube clip of Huckabee's response can be seen at www.youtube.com/watch?v=n-BFEhkIujA (accessed March 7, 2008).

WHEN I WANT YOUR OPINION, I'LL BEAT IT OUT OF YOU

One of my favorite posters is an extreme close-up of a gorilla with the caption "When I want your opinion, I'll beat it out of you." Sometimes it's like that with creation and evolution. People who really don't want to hear your

HARD TO TRY THIS AT HOME

Maybe you've heard the one about the agnostic who was arguing with God about how life came about. Having studied the theory of how a primordial soup of protein-rich ooze was sparked by lightning to produce life, the agnostic said to God, "Eh, no big deal, I bet I can do that."

The Lord said, "OK, give it your best shot."

So the agnostic started to scoop up some dirt.

"No, no," God said. "Get your own dirt."

opinion start thumping their chests and acting overly aggressive if you don't assume a submissive attitude.

Unfortunately, you can't always tell where you stand with people right off the bat. That's why I've put together the diagrams shared in this chapter. They'll help you figure out

- *where people are coming from;*
- *why they're coming from where they're coming from; and*
- *how to start building bridges with people you might not agree with on everything, but can on some things.*

Overall, the main thing is to keep the main thing as the main thing. As Jesus said, that main thing is to come into a relationship with God, to glorify him with our lives and our love for him, and to love our neighbors as ourselves (Matthew 22:37-39). One might even say that will lead to enjoying him forever.

Sometimes when we're in the middle of the creation/evolution debate we forget the most important things.

05 THEMISSINGLINK

The grass withers and the flowers fall, but the word of our God stands forever.
—ISAIAH, OLD TESTAMENT PROPHET, ABOUT SEVEN HUNDRED
YEARS BEFORE JESUS (ISAIAH 40:8)

I tell you the truth, until heaven and earth disappear, not the smallest letter, not the least stroke of a pen, will by any means disappear from the Law until everything is accomplished.
—JESUS (MATTHEW 5:18)

All Scripture is God-breathed.
—THE APOSTLE PAUL (2 TIMOTHY 3:16)

Normally, when people think of missing links they're thinking about gaps in the fossil record between one species and another or, say, a common ancestor to apes and humans.

In this chapter, the missing link is the unanimous voice that Christians ought to have about the inspiration, authority, and missionary nature of God's Word, a harmony that often gets lost in the creation/evolution tussle.

BOTTOM LINE: **PEOPLE SAY A LOT OF NEGATIVE STUFF ABOUT THE BIBLE** THAT AIN'T NECESSARILY SO.

Whichever option we take on creation and evolution, we need to respect the message and authority of God's Word. Too often people take a cavalier attitude toward the Bible that says it's a book that is just old-fashioned, culturally conditioned, time-bound, or full of mistakes. As a result, they might say we don't need to take it that seriously. "What mistakes?" you might ask? Well, here are just a few that some people claim:

- *That Genesis 2 contradicts Genesis 1 (which is not true and imposes a bunch of invalid assumptions on the text).*

- *That the Bible puts the earth at the center of the universe (which some Christians in history have believed, even though the Bible does not actually seek to address this topic).*

- *That the book of Leviticus is made up of nothing but a bunch of strange rules (many of which do seem that way to us today, from the perspective of 2,000 years of Christian hindsight).*

Bottom line: people say a lot of negative stuff about the Bible that ain't necessarily so.

So before we go any further, we need to talk about upholding the integrity of the Bible. It isn't just a human book, a mere relic from ancient history, or simply an expression of elevated religious sentiments. It's God's Word. We can't be flip about it.

At the least, this means we need to give the Bible the benefit of the doubt and give it a chance to speak God's Word to us personally. If we go into a Scripture passage trying to pull it apart and nitpick over our personal pet peeves, we're not allowing ourselves to be open to what God is trying to say.

It's important that we let it speak to us on its own terms, rather than shove *ours* onto it.

What follows are some thoughts on how to do just that.

THE BIBLE IS ANCIENT LITERATURE

The Bible was not written a few years ago, not written in our language, and not penned in our cultural context. It comes to us as a series of books, collected over a period of about 1,400 years, written by many authors from quite a few different cultures. It comes to us in three languages and the conventions and grammar of those languages (Hebrew and Aramaic in the Old Testament and Greek in the New Testament). And it comes to us in different literary forms: historical narratives, law codes, poetry, drama, wisdom sayings and proverbs, social critique, prophesies, apocalyptic warnings, gospels, doctrinal teachings, and in letters to both churches and individuals.

Each of these factors needs to be taken into account if we want to accomplish two very important goals:

- *Try to discern what the various Bible sections meant to the people reading them at the time.*

- *Seek to determine what significance they have for us today.*

Uncovering the intent of the authors is key. In Bible interpretation this means two things: we want to try to understand both the human authors' intent (even if we don't know who the human authors were) and the divine author's intent (the source of inspiration for the human authors). To do this, we need to try to always take into account the overall message of each Bible book as well as how each book contributes to the gradual, yet progressive, development of God's revelation as a whole.

THE BIBLE IS AUTHORITATIVE, INSPIRED SCRIPTURE

We also want to keep in mind that the Bible's distinct view of inspiration is totally different from, say, that of the Koran, the holy book of Islam. According to Islam, a perfect Koran is in Heaven and Mohammad was told to read or "recite" it (*Koran* literally means "recitation"). In contrast, in the biblical writings,

THE UNSTATED ASSUMPTION IS THAT **NO CORRECT OR VALID INTERPRETATION IS POSSIBLE** BECAUSE EACH OF US CREATES MEANING TO THE TEXT WHEN WE READ IT.

the human authors wrote both from revelation and from their own experiences, using their own faculties. The inspiration of the Holy Spirit was upon them and guiding what they wrote (see 2 Peter 1:20, 21). But that inspiration didn't negate their human contribution to the finished work.

The Bible's intended message is both hidden and open. It remains hidden to those unwilling to submit their hearts to God, but it is open to all who want to love God and put his Word into practice in their lives. As important as it is to apply our reason to sifting, weighing, and analyzing what the Bible says, we also need illumination from the Holy Spirit to really "get it." The Bible itself encourages us to ask God to show us, to cry out to him for wisdom (James 1:5; Proverbs 2:1-9). If we do our part, God promises to give us his wisdom. But wisdom doesn't mean having all the answers. It means rightly applying God's truth to our lives.

THE BIBLE AND ITS INTERPRETERS

When matters of biblical interpretation come up, it's become fashionable for people to say, "Oh, that's just *your* interpretation." The unstated assumption is that no correct or valid interpretation is possible because each of us creates meaning to the text when we read it.

There is some truth to this because all of us are limited in our abilities and experiences, but it's based in false humility and creates a huge amount of weasel room for us to evade anything that the Bible clearly says. So what's a better approach?

Aristotle said, "Know thyself." This is good advice, in general, because nobody comes to the Bible as a completely blank slate; each of us brings our own culture, background, and baggage as we read. We have our own expectations about grammar and how words are used. We're accustomed to our own culture's literary conventions and styles that aren't the same as the Bible's. In addition, we have our own life situations, problems, intents, interests, and yes, agendas that we bring to the table.

Therefore, going into our Bible reading and Bible study, we want to be aware of both the social, intellectual, and cultural horizon of the Bible's authors, as well as our own. We want to take a stance of humility, asking God to show us what he wants us to know and do. We want to make sure that we really listen to the best minds of God's people through the ages. And we want to listen to what Christians are saying, not just in our denominational or geographical corner of the world, but in other places as well. This doesn't mean that everybody's equally right, but at least we're positioning ourselves so that we can do a little self-questioning and self-correcting.

We need to get the main message of the Bible before we move to the more obscure things. Let's apply this principle to a couple of Jew-Gentile problems from the New Testament church.

THE BIBLE FOCUSES ON THE MAJORS

Example #1: A bone of contention in the early church was whether it was acceptable to eat meat that had been sacrificed to idols. The Jews didn't do this; the Gentiles did. How could peace prevail in a church that included both Jews and Gentiles? It was a complicated cross-cultural and cross-religious issue.

The apostle Paul picked up that bone and seized the opportunity to beat some narrow-minded people over the head with it. Essentially, he said, this is a disputable matter, something that individuals need to follow their own consciences about, something that people can disagree over. Each one has to make up his or her own mind, but each one needs to cut some slack to those who take up another practice. The overall goal, he was saying, is to promote peace and unity in the new body of Christ, the church. In other words, passing judgment on others is out; love is in.[61] Whatever we do, it ought to be for the glory of God so others can come to know Jesus.

> ARISTOTLE SAID, "KNOW THYSELF." THIS IS GOOD ADVICE, IN GENERAL, BECAUSE NOBODY COMES TO THE BIBLE AS A COMPLETELY BLANK SLATE.

THE BIBLE AS A MISSIONARY BOOK

Example #2: Another big question arose in the early church. It dealt with whether Gentiles should be required to go through a two-step process of becoming believers in Jesus (both accepting the gospel *and* being circumcised), rather than one.

In Acts 15 some Jewish-Christian teachers claimed that if the Gentile believers wanted to be saved, they would have to be circumcised—in other words, come under the entire Mosaic law. This might have been the practice of Jewish missionaries before Jesus, but would the new church do things the same way? The question was brought to a council of Jesus' disciples and major leaders in Jerusalem, the headquarters of the early church. Since all the decision makers were Jews by heritage, one might have thought the deck was stacked in favor of the teachers from Judea and Antioch.

However, the Jerusalem council opened their arms to the Gentiles and welcomed them as full brothers and sisters in Christ without forcing them to become Jews in their physical bodies. It was an act of amazing grace and wisdom. James, the brother of Jesus and most likely the leader of the church in Jerusalem at the time, insightfully declared: "It is my judgment, therefore, that we should not make it difficult for the Gentiles who are turning to God" (Acts 15:19). In effect, James was saying, "Let's not put unnecessary obstacles in the way of people who want to follow Jesus."

THE BIBLE IS SELF-AUTHENTICATING

The Holy Spirit inspired the Bible. Therefore, the Bible needs no outside authorities pronouncing it valid or giving it their seal of approval. It is self-authenticating.

In Jewish-Christian history, this hasn't always been understood. The Pharisees of Jesus' time felt they had to build a hedge around the law, so they came up with hundreds of extra little laws to protect people in the community from *even coming close* to breaking God's laws. Jesus devastatingly critiqued this approach in his Sermon on the Mount (Matthew 5–7).

The post–New Testament church fell into a similar trap. Soon after the apostles died, a hierarchical priesthood developed with ceremonial clothing, ornate and fixed worship patterns, and a denial of the priesthood of all believers, which was God's original intent (see Exodus 19:6 and 1 Peter 2:5, 9). The second- and third-century church was essentially saying, "The Bible's self-authenticating inspiration is not enough. We need all this other stuff."

THE BIBLE AS GOD'S WORD DESERVES RESPECT

So what do meat sacrificed to idols, circumcision, and building hedges around the law have to do with the Late Great Ape Debate?

Plenty. They're reminders that whatever else happens, we need to keep focused on what we earlier called the white-hot core of Christian faith. Therefore, first, let's cut each other slack on disputable matters; second, let's avoid throwing roadblocks in people's way that obstruct them from finding Jesus; and third, let's not put hedges around God's Word or make it subservient to science.

Whatever we think about creation and evolution, God's Word speaks the truth because God *is* truth; God's Word aligns with reality because God *is* reality; God's Word can be trusted because God is faithful; God's Word communicates to us personally through our spirits because God is an infinite and personal spirit; and God's Word will not pass away, because God is durable.

> SO WHAT DO **MEAT SACRIFICED TO IDOLS, CIRCUMCISION, AND BUILDING HEDGES AROUND THE LAW** HAVE TO DO WITH THE LATE GREAT APE DEBATE?

A RUMBLE IN THE JUNGLE

06 THEREVOLUTIONOFEVOLUTION

That which struck the present writer most forcibly on his first perusal of [On the] Origin of Species *was the conviction that Teleology, as commonly understood, had received its deathblow at Mr. Darwin's hands.*
—T. H. HUXLEY, BIOLOGIST, ANSWERING DARWIN'S CRITICS (1860)

Violent, irrational, intolerant, allied to racism and tribalism and bigotry, invested in ignorance and hostile to free inquiry, contemptuous of women and coercive toward children: organized religion ought to have a great deal on its conscience.
—CHRISTOPHER HITCHENS, AUTHOR OF *GOD IS NOT GREAT: HOW RELIGION POISONS EVERYTHING* (2007)

TELEOLOGY: The study of the evidences of design or purpose in nature.

Well, it's pretty clear which side of the fence Christopher Hitchens is on! He's not just firing his verbal attacks at Christianity; his guns are turned on religion everywhere and anywhere.

No doubt in many cases religious people have earned Hitchens's anger. But we need to see his militant atheistic attitude as part of a larger cultural story in which we find ourselves. Some agree with Hitchens 100 percent and want to make him out to be something of a hero on a triumphant march. Others can't figure out why God has to be thrown out the window just because you disagree in the whole creation/evolution debate. Still others would call his views nothing less than out-and-out lies.

Wherever you may be coming from, this chapter seeks to set evolution's revolution within the context of this larger story. It tackles the question, how could the theory of evolution become so convincing to so many people?

To put our arms around the subject, we'll briefly survey how Christianity became the dominant player in Western culture; recall a series of major revolutions (I'll call them cage-rattlings) that challenged the church's standing and authority; then look at Darwinism's impact on science.

For readers who love history, the following survey will come off as vastly oversimplified. I apologize in advance. But if you only have one chapter to cover 2,000 years of history, what can you do?

MONKEYS ON A STRING: THE MEDIEVAL SYNTHESIS

Christianity began as a persecuted offshoot of first-century Judaism. But in relatively quick time, it crossed the cultural threshold from Jewish into pagan, polytheistic (many gods) Greco-Roman society. After a little less than 300 years, it had become strong enough that, in the early part of the fourth century, the Roman Emperor Constantine converted to Christianity and took his empire with him. In Western civilization, from that time until the

DARWINISM: The theory of biological evolution, developed by Charles Darwin and others, that says all species of organisms arise and develop through the natural selection of small, inherited genetic variations.

American Revolution, Christianity in some form was the official religion, receiving patronage, perks, and power from the state.

As Christianity expanded into new cultural basins, the educated class was populated greatly by monks, nuns, and other clergy. In effect, the church had a monopoly on knowledge. *Monopoly* here doesn't mean that everybody believed exactly the same things. Far from it. But everything was discussed and debated within the context of faith and Christian religion. In the Western church, centered in Rome, the pope and ruling bishops (called the magisterium) became the ultimate deciders in religious and moral matters.

At times, the popes and bishops even fixed things to put themselves into positions of immense secular power.

IN WESTERN CIVILIZATION, FROM THAT TIME UNTIL THE AMERICAN REVOLUTION, **CHRISTIANITY IN SOME FORM WAS THE OFFICIAL RELIGION,** RECEIVING PATRONAGE, PERKS, AND POWER FROM THE STATE.

Meanwhile, over a thousand-year period, Christian thinkers and philosophers developed what's since been termed the medieval synthesis, a set of beliefs about the world and humanity's place in it. They didn't reactively and unthinkingly reject everything in polytheistic philosophy, but instead allowed some of it to seep into their beliefs.

Included in this set of beliefs was the idea of a geocentric universe. Members of the church had gotten this idea from Aristotle (384–322 BC), a very insightful Greek philosopher and an almost unimpeachable source in the medieval synthesis, along with astronomer and scientist Ptolemy (about 150 BC) after him. According to geocentrism, the earth stood still in a central position in the universe; the stars were fixed points of light in "the firmament," which was considered a shell-like or tent-like structure within which the sun, moon, and planets moved around the earth; and the firmament held back heavenly waters, which if loosed could destroy everything very quickly.

This cosmology could also be described, in terms of space, as a three-tiered universe. People literally thought of God, the angels, and Heaven as "up" and "above"; the earth as "in the middle"; and Hell, Sheol, and the demons as "down" and "below."[62]

COSMOLOGY: The study of the form, content, organization, and origins of the universe, whether the study be scientific, religious, philosophical, or cultural.

The medieval synthesis sought to take into account science as it was known at the time, but much of the science of the period was based more on speculation and on what respected authorities said, rather than on measurable data. From our perspective in the twenty-first century, the medieval synthesis carried a lot of superstitious ideas.

Beyond cosmology, the medieval synthesis kept everyone on a fairly tight string. It saw social relations as ordered by God. Theocracy was assumed. Kings reigned as representatives of God; they supported the church and the church supported the king. Great deference to authority was required, and rulers saw religious dissent as a veiled or direct threat to the state. In the pecking order, bloodlines, heredity, and class were presumed to be ordained by God and therefore unchangeable. Women were considered second-class or even slave property. Serfs had no opportunity to improve their lot. Slavery was tolerated.

As we evaluate the medieval synthesis, we can probably discern some good and bad. We need to realize that it was only one interpretation of the biblical worldview; it was not the biblical worldview itself. The medieval synthesis respected God's Word and the gospel message that God so loved his world that he sent his Son into it to save us from our sins. It affirmed that God has a design and a purpose for everything he does. But it also had a lot of add-ons. It may have been a reasonable approximation of the biblical worldview based on people's limited perspectives and experience at the time, but it definitely left room for improvement.

RATTLING THE CAGE #1: DISPLACING THE CHURCH

In the sixteenth century, the Protestant Reformation posed a sweeping challenge to the medieval church's dominating influence over religion, politics, economics, philosophy, and education.

Martin Luther (1483–1546), an Augustinian monk, loyal son of the Roman Catholic Church, and college theology professor, began to realize that the Catholic Church was teaching and doing certain things that went against the clear teaching of Scripture. To protest and bring these wrongs out into the open, in 1517 he nailed his famous Ninety-Five Theses on the Wittenberg Cathedral door. Luther's debating points spread like wildfire throughout Germany and the rest of northern Europe. He was calling into question some of the most foundational assumptions on which the Catholic hierarchy—and Western civilization—were based.

> THE MEDIEVAL SYNTHESIS AFFIRMED THAT **GOD HAS A DESIGN AND A PURPOSE** FOR EVERYTHING HE DOES. BUT IT ALSO HAD A LOT OF ADD-ONS.

Luther and the other Reformers claimed that the heart of the gospel was salvation by grace through faith rather than by faith *plus* good works *plus* the sacraments *plus* whatever extras the church required. They shouted that what Christ did for us on the cross was the main thing, not church rituals. Authority came from Scripture alone, not church traditions and power structures.

To steer people back to the authority of the Scriptures, the Reformers started translating the Bible into the languages of the day and publishing the Bible for mass consumption. Before Luther and the other Reformers, there were no teen study Bibles, no copies of *The Message* lying around in students' rooms. Very few had their own copies of the Bible to read for themselves.

Luther and the Reformers believed the Bible's message was so clear that regular people could read and interpret the Scriptures for themselves, as opposed to the Roman Catholic Church practice of locking up religious knowledge in Latin and allowing only highly educated Catholic scholars and clergy access to the Bible. Against the Roman Catholic idea that priesthood was vested in the clergy, the Reformers taught the priesthood of all believers (a clear biblical teaching, in 1 Peter 2:5, 9), thus dignifying the daily work of people who labored in fields other than religion.

The Reformation was a radical, insurrection-like project. Many of the Reformers called the Catholic Church a false church and worse. Religious wars ensued. Things got very messy.

Luther had kick-started a breakaway movement from Catholic authority. He had unleashed a radical idea, putting his own individual conscience, bound by loyalty to the Scriptures, above the authority of the Roman Catholic Church and the pope. People had been burned at the stake for less.

> LUTHER HAD KICK-STARTED A BREAKAWAY MOVEMENT FROM CATHOLIC AUTHORITY. **PEOPLE HAD BEEN BURNED AT THE STAKE FOR LESS.**

But Luther and the other Reformers did not have the last word on knowing or applying the biblical worldview. Theirs was an important contribution and clarification of some core Christian truths, and as an overall project it was their best effort at putting forth the biblical worldview as they knew it. But the Reformers still lacked a good deal of science, and many of them still held to the church-state pattern that had been in vogue since Constantine. And yet, by putting freedom of conscience above the authority of the Catholic Church on religious matters, they opened the door for challenging the church in other fields of knowledge as well.

RATTLING THE CAGE #2: DEMOTING THE EARTH

Nicolaus Copernicus (1473–1543), a complete Renaissance man and expert in many fields—including law, philosophy, theology, and medicine—was a contemporary of Luther. He was also a Roman Catholic bishop and astronomer. His book *On the Revolutions of the Celestial Spheres*, overturning an Earth-centered universe and advocating a heliocentric (or sun-centered) universe, was published in the year of his death.

GALILEO GALILEI: A Tuscan (Italy) physicist, mathematician, astronomer, and philosopher. He has been called the father of modern observational astronomy and the father of modern science, among other unofficial titles. He was a devout Roman Catholic.

Copernicus didn't get in trouble with the religious establishment for his views. But the Italian Galileo Galilei (1564–1642), a brash and uncompromising figure, did. Galileo pioneered precise, quantitative experiments and direct observations that corroborated Copernicus's heliocentric model. He was the first person to train a telescope on Jupiter and notice its moons.

Perhaps because of his personality, perhaps because the Protestant Reformation had made the Catholic authorities more nervous about any challenge to their authority, Galileo got in a lot of trouble for his discoveries. He was even brought up on charges of heresy, which could have led to a death penalty. This was serious business!

FUN WITH JUPITER: What Galileo did with Jupiter, you can do with binoculars. On a clear, dark night, find Jupiter in the sky and fix your binoculars on it. If you're lucky, four moons will appear in a plane that bisects the middle of the planet. Come back a couple of hours later, and you'll notice the moons have moved.

Why was Galileo so dangerous? Galileo flat-out said the Roman Catholic Church was wrong about the earth being the center of the universe and had been wrong for a very long time. The error began with big-name church fathers like Origen, Ambrose, and Augustine.[63] Who was Galileo to disagree?

The Inquisition brought Galileo up on charges of heresy. In 1633 the papal sentence (a statement of condemnation) of Galileo's teaching came down:

The proposition that the Sun is the center of the world and does not move from its place is absurd and false philosophically and formally heretical, because it is expressly contrary to Holy Scripture.[64]

This was a classic case of the Roman Catholic Church using hardball tactics to protect its turf. It's also a classic example of the church inappropriately tying doctrine to a particular scientific theory.

In the short term, the inquisitors made Galileo recant his views. He had to live the rest of his life under house arrest, turning his formidable talents in other scientific directions. But as time passed and the heliocentric model became more and more persuasive, the Galileo trial made the Catholic Church look bad. In 1741—a little more than a century after the papal sentence—the church reversed course, allowing Galileo's work to be published. In 1758 it removed a prohibition it had ordered against teaching the heliocentric view. Finally, in 1992, 359 years after the Galileo incident, Pope John Paul II formally expressed regret for how the case was handled.[65]

RATTLING THE CAGE #3: GEOLOGY AND DEEP TIME

For the Catholic Church, the Galileo hit was disturbing, but not devastating. So what if the sun, moon, and planets moved according to laws of gravitation (instead of being directly pushed along by God)? God was still the mind behind gravity. Not an insurmountable problem.

Geology hit closer to home.

Until the eighteenth century, the world was mainly seen as either eternal—going through a series of births and rebirths (as taught by Aristotle)—or that it had a beginning and an end and was only a few thousand years old. The conventional wisdom for the second view was that creation happened somewhere around 4000 BC.

The Anglo-Irish archbishop James Ussher (sometimes spelled Usher) was so intrigued by the issue that he amassed a 10,000-volume library, in many languages, on the subject.

Ussher correlated the biblical genealogies with the best dates he could find from nonbiblical sources, and in *The Annals of the New Testament* (published in 1650), on the first page, he published the following news:

In the beginning, God created heaven and earth, which beginning of time, according to this chronology, occurred at the beginning of the night which preceded the 23rd of October in the year 710 of the Julian period [4004 BC by the Western calendar]. [66]

JAMES USSHER: Anglican archbishop of Ireland who was a prolific scholar and famously published a chronology of dates that placed the earth's date of birth as in October 4004 BC.

Not long after this, James Lightfoot, the vice chancellor of Cambridge University, chanced to correct Ussher's findings. He adjusted zero-hour to the year 4004 BC on October 26—at 9 o'clock in the morning!

As a result of the work of these two scholars, the year 4004 BC gained a lot of credibility. It attained near-iconic status with the advent of marginal notes in Bibles, and for generations 4004 BC was confidently affixed as the year in which the Trinity created the heavens and the earth. As a sign of cultural influence, well into the 1970s the Gideon Bibles placed in hotel rooms added "4004 BC" next to Genesis 1:1. In this chapter, we'll call this "the traditional view."

> AS A RESULT OF THE WORK OF THESE TWO SCHOLARS, **THE YEAR 4004 BC GAINED A LOT OF CREDIBILITY.** IT ATTAINED NEAR-ICONIC STATUS.

However, not long after Ussher and Lightfoot, the infant discipline of geology began to stir. One of the first people to look at rocks, fossils, and time as a single, coherent story was a Scotsman, James Hutton (1726-1797). A naturalist, chemist, farmer, and the father of modern geology, Hutton paid close attention to landscapes. He wondered about the huge deposits of white chalk, and why some fossils could be found only in certain places but not in others. Rather than thinking forward from an ancient, unknown point, Hutton did a revolutionary thing: he started with the earth as it is and tried to work back in time from the present moment.

As a farmer, Hutton noticed the slow destruction of land by streams carrying sediment to the sea. He reasoned that the soil in the streams must have come from higher hills and mountains, where the effects of frost, wind, and rain had reduced larger boulders to smaller and smaller rocks, mud, and silt. He also noticed that plains have lots of good topsoil, representing the silt that rivers had laid down over time.

He further reasoned that, taken out to sea, the river-loads of silt would eventually be deposited, pressured by the weight of more layers, consolidated, and turned into solid rock. In this way, new continents could form even as old ones eroded. Hutton didn't know what forces in the earth had caused the lifting and folding of sea layers into mountains, but he had a hunch it might have something to do with volcanoes and magma under the earth.

HUTTON SPECULATED THAT A HUGE AMOUNT OF TIME WOULD BE NEEDED TO ACCOMPLISH THESE THINGS, SO HE WENT ABOUT LOOKING FOR OUTSTANDING EXAMPLES OF HIS THEORY.

Hutton speculated that a huge amount of time would be needed to accomplish these things, so he went about looking for outstanding examples of his theory. He believed he found one. Near Jedburgh, in a bank cut by a stream, he found an accordion-like sedimentary outcrop of rock, the creases tilted vertically. On top of them he found a layer of cobbles. On top of those he found sedimentary layers of flat-lying sandstone, and on top of those sat a beautiful Scottish countryside scene with grass and trees growing in the topsoil.

Hutton had found what geologists now call an angular unconformity: evidence of a world in decay (the present), sitting on the ruins of a earlier world in decay (the sandstone and cobbles), which itself was sitting on the ruins of another world which had decayed. It was an amazing, startling picture. When Hutton and a colleague, John Playfair, found a similar outcrop at a coastal headlands at Siccar Point, Playfair wrote of growing "giddy" by looking far into the "abyss of time."

A vivid illustration of the possibility of deep time sticks in my mind from my honeymoon in Bar Harbor, Maine (the locals call it Bah Hahbah). My new bride and I decided to go on a geology walk with a ranger-naturalist. How romantic, right?

Anyway, this guy in his olive-green campaign hat took a group of us down to the beach and used a walking stick to draw a long line in the sand. It was about the length of a football field. Then we started to walk, and he started to make some marks. About thirty yards from the end zone, he said, "Here's our first evidence for single-cell animals, bacteria, and the like." Then he walked off about fifty yards and said, "Here's where the first multi-celled creatures appear." Another ten yards and he told us that the first land plants were beginning at this point. We were about ten yards from the opposite goal line and we hadn't even gotten to the dinosaurs! About seven and a half yards out, the first land animals showed up; a yard more represented the first winged insects, amphibians, and reptiles. Another couple of feet and the seas filled with fish. At the five-yard line, the dinosaurs and mammals arrived at last, but at two and a half yards, the dinosaurs went extinct. About two inches from the end of the line, he told us, were where the earliest hominid (erect, two-footed mammals) ancestors came on the scene. Spaced in the rest of those two inches, he said, was Neanderthal man; the Neolithic period; the Egyptian, Babylonian, Greek, and Roman civilizations; Christopher Columbus; and the American Revolution.

The ranger's walk-and-talk wasn't science in and of itself, of course, but his way of illustrating what many geologists have said. It was an unsettling experience for me and hard to dovetail with the traditional view.

RATTLING THE CAGE #4: EVOLUTION'S REVOLUTION

The Reformation, astronomy, and geology had set the stage for Darwin. The story is legendary: his voyage for five years with the HMS *Beagle*, the isolated Galapagos Islands, his analytical tools, comparative anatomy, and more. (See "Darwin at Sea.") Upon his return to England, and in consultation with other experts, he crunched an immense amount of data and intuitively came up with a grand thesis, proposing that over long periods of time, living things change; that change affects their body shape, functions, behavior, and how they interact with their environment; and that underlying all change is hereditary material that alters from one generation to the next. Darwin didn't know what the heredity mechanism was; that discovery would be left to others.

DARWIN AT SEA: In 1831, Charles Darwin boarded the HMS *Beagle* as a 23-year-old student clergyman and amateur naturalist. The trip originally was planned to take two years. It took five. What Darwin discovered along the way would forever change science.

The film *Master and Commander: The Far Side of the World* (2003) gives us a playful and tantalizing glimpse of a gifted and curious naturalist on the verge of a great discovery at the Galapagos Islands in about 1805 (the time of the Napoleonic wars)—but who is foiled by the appearance of a French warship.

Fortunately for Darwin, the time frame was three decades later, hostilities with the French had eased, the *Beagle* was not charged with war (but with a reconnaissance mission along the South American coasts), and he was free to make lengthy excursions on land and liberally collect specimens. His stay at the Galapagos Islands (a string of volcanic islands west of Ecuador, in the Pacific Ocean), while only a month long, was not cut short.

Darwin had a real Indiana Jones–type adventure. He rode with Argentinian gauchos, got waylaid in an insurrection, and climbed to the top of the Andes Mountains—all the while avidly collecting his samples. He unearthed sensational specimens of extinct giant mammals. He found living species that had been unknown in Europe at the time. He collected thousands of fossils and examples of flora and fauna. At various ports along the way, Darwin would send his collections back to Cambridge (his university back in England), along with his detailed journals. Even before his voyage ended, Darwin had set the scientific establishment in England astir. When he finally returned, scientists honored him as a hero.

But even though his journals show the beginnings of doubt about "the stability of species" early on, it took Darwin another twenty-three years to publish *On the Origin of Species.* And that came only after Alfred Russell Wallace—another naturalist whose own theory about species generation was very similar to Darwin's—looked like he was about to scoop Darwin and get credit for the theory.

NATURAL SELECTION: According to Darwinian theory, only the organisms best adapted to their environment tend to survive and transmit their genetic characteristics in increasing numbers to succeeding generations; those less adapted are eliminated.

Darwin's theory had revolutionary impact. Like him or not, right or wrong, since *On the Origin of Species* came out, Darwin's theory has been racking up an impressive series of wins in the scientific community. The principles he described, his language of evolution through natural selection and transmutation, and his proposal that all of life derives from a common ancestor (or set of similar ancestors) are the foundations for—and have driven advances in—all the biological sciences.

RATTLING THE CAGE #5: THE EVIDENCE OF THE FOSSILS

Before Hutton, for thousands of years, people had been digging up fossils and didn't quite know what to make of them. Were fossils animals that had been somehow stranded and turned to stone? Had they grown from seeds? Were they pranks of the devil to deceive the faithful? Were the curled bivalve fossils scattered all over Europe really "the devil's toenails," as the folklore of the time suggested? Were fossils of supernatural, or magical, origin?

Christians had long assumed that most fossils came from Noah's flood, including marine fossils found in the mountains. But not everyone bought that idea. Leonardo da Vinci (1452–1519) voiced his skepticism, pointing out the great distance between the sea and the Apennine Mountains in which fossil clams had been found.

Since Hutton, the field of geology has sharpened and grown as the fragmentary fossil record has been better pieced together. Here's a brief explanation.

We now know that fossils are the remains of ancient animals and plants embedded in rocks. Scientists have pieced together the following clues to their meaning: Fossils are only found in certain places and in certain kinds of rocks; fossils are not scattered randomly, but tell a consistent story; fossils are the closest thing we have to a time machine into the past.

From the fossil record most scientists who study these things have concluded that, over time, new forms of life have arisen from older forms; that simpler life forms dominated earlier periods of the earth's history and more complex forms are relatively recent; that massive extinctions have occurred; and that some species, once widespread and plentiful, are no longer among us.

Hutton had begun to employ fossils in his ideas, but William Smith took knowledge of fossils to a new level. As a canal digger in Britain, he noticed and catalogued similar sequences of layered rock (and types of fossils in those layers) in different parts of the country. In 1815 Smith brought all his data together visually for the first time in a colored geologic map of the island nation. His amazing diagram changed our view of the earth for all time. It tells the story of a continuous "geologic column," a series of geologic events that can be traced in rock and linked by fossils.[67]

Smith's contribution has inspired several new scientific fields of study to understand the surface of the earth. As a result, geologists, paleontologists, and others have found that the earth's crust is not motionless, but tremendously active. They've discovered the mechanism for uplifting sea fossils to the tops of mountains, called plate tectonics and continental drift. They've documented that the earth's crust sits on a sea of slowly churning, molten lava. Over eons of time, scientists say, entire continents crash into each other, sections of continents are gobbled up by sea trenches, and in places the seafloor itself is spreading and pushing continents away from each other. Today, geologic findings are cross-checked by things like rock strata, plant and animal fossils, uranium isotope dating, and volcanic ash in far-spread locations. By these means, scientists from many disciplines have concluded that the earth is about 4.5 billion years old.

FOR THOUSANDS OF YEARS, PEOPLE HAD BEEN DIGGING UP FOSSILS AND DIDN'T QUITE KNOW WHAT TO MAKE OF THEM. WERE FOSSILS ANIMALS THAT HAD BEEN SOMEHOW STRANDED AND TURNED TO STONE?

Clearly this challenges Ussher's traditional view. Anti-evolutionists respond: "This is speculation. If evolution is true, why are transitional fossils (of in-between species) missing?" Scientists answer that even though the fossil evidence is indeed incomplete, as more and more evidence is gathered, many of those previously "missing" transitional slots keep getting filled. A Theistic Evolution scientist like Francis Collins will argue that the ages of these fossilized organisms can be accurately estimated by measuring the radioactive decay of various elements over time.[68]

Two examples are archaeopteryx, an animal said to bridge the gap between reptiles (some get more specific by saying dinosaurs) and birds; and tiktaalik, an animal said to be the link between fishes and tetrapods (animals having four limbs). The first archaeopteryx fossil was found in 1865; the latest (and tenth) was discovered in 2005. The first tiktaalik fossil was discovered, a team of scientists said, in Arctic Canada in April 2006. Evolutionary scientists would say that both archaeopteryx and tiktaalik are precisely the kinds of transitional forms or "missing links" that Darwin's theory would lead us to expect.[69]

Creationists and anti-evolutionists respond that the archaeopteryx was a complete bird and thus could not be transitional; the same type of argument is made regarding the tiktaalik.

Regarding the stickier issue of human evolution, Francisco J. Ayala, once an ordained Dominican priest and now a biological scientist at the University of California–Irvine, shared his perspective:

> The missing link is no longer missing. Not one, but hundreds of fossil remains belonging to hundreds of individual hominids have been discovered since Darwin's time and continue to be discovered at an accelerated rate.[70]

He then goes on to name a slew of them.[71] Scientists across many disciplines would ask this question: If newer finds keep filling out the fossil record with what they see as greater precision and the "gaps" keep getting narrower, what happens to the "lack of transitional fossils" argument?

RATTLING THE CAGE #6: STARLIGHT AND THE EXPANDING UNIVERSE

Starlight from deep space causes another problem for the traditional creation date. At night we're constantly pelted by light waves and particles from burning fireballs out there in space. If the universe were only 6,000 years old, then the only light we should be receiving on a dark night would be from a few lonely nearby stars within a 6,000-light-year bubble. Any other light photons or waves (or infrared light, X-rays, microwaves, and "background" cosmic radiation left over from the Big Bang) beyond that threshold—the vast majority of what scientists see and measure—would be beyond what we should be able to see because they wouldn't have had time to get here.

What explanations have proponents of the traditional view offered to rebut these arguments? Option #1: Those faraway stars and galaxies do exist, but light is not a constant. It's slowing down over time. (Mainstream science does not accept this explanation.) Option #2: Those faraway stars and galaxies do exist, but God miraculously "warp-speeds" their light and energy waves to us so we can see them, which we couldn't otherwise. Option #3: Those faraway stars and galaxies don't actually exist, but God continually creates photons from those nonexistent galaxies to make us think they are there.

Backers of these options might acknowledge they don't have the perfect answer for the difficulties raised by each, or they might suggest that "the science is not yet in" and much remains to be discovered. But to put it charitably, for many people working in this field of science, the three explanations offered above sound forced.

Also, since Galileo, our view of the universe has expanded exponentially. We've gone from believing that the earth is one planet among several to one among many; from the sun as the only huge burning fireball to the sun as one of hundreds of billions in our galaxy; from our solar system as the center of the universe to our solar system as existing toward the edge of a spiral-shaped galaxy, of which there are hundreds of billions; from a universe that is static and about 6,000 years old to a universe that is expanding and about 15 billion years old.

RATTLING THE CAGE #7: GREGOR MENDEL AND GENETICS

Darwin's theory of natural selection was captivating to many, but the great mystery in his theory was how incremental changes occur in plants and animals, giving them a competitive edge for survival. Today, Darwin's theory, plus genetic studies, are combined in what is often called neo-Darwinism.

So what is this genetic thing all about?

In 1865 Gregor Mendel, an Augustinian monk tending peas in what is now the Czech Republic, discovered that "children" peas got their genetic material from their "parents." He devised experiments to statistically predict outcomes of breeding different characteristics, such as peas with wrinkled or smooth appearances. Building on Mendel's work, in 1944 three different scientists[xii] proved that DNA, not proteins (as previously thought), carried the genetic information.

DNA: Deoxyribonucleic acid: an extremely long macromolecule that is the main component of chromosomes and is the material that transfers genetic characteristics in all life forms; it is constructed of two strands coiled around each other in a ladder-like arrangement.

Then in 1953, James Watson and Francis Crick deduced that the DNA molecule was an elegantly simple double helix— a twisted ladder of chemical codes. Because of Watson and Crick's dramatic discovery, we now know that inside the cell's nucleus, DNA is densely packed into chromosomes in the form of threadlike linear strands. DNA acts like a software program that tells the cell what to do. DNA has a coding language of four "letters" (think of them as chemical signatures) that occur in "base pairs" (A, which can only be paired with C; and G, which can only be paired with T). Each gene (or coding instruction) takes up hundreds of thousands of letters of DNA code. Every living thing on the planet is governed by this simple language,

[xii] Oswald T. Avery, Colin M. MacLeod, and Maclyn McCarty

GENOMES, CHROMOSOMES, AND MUTATIONS: For the record, humans have twenty-three chromosomes in their sex cells, about 20,000 protein-producing (essentially "functioning") genes, and 3.1 billion base pairs of genetic code—enough for a stack of books as high as the Washington Monument.

In 2003 the decade-long Human Genome Project to map the entire 3.1 billion base pairs of the human genome was completed. It was a magnificent scientific achievement that already is yielding a treasure-trove of results. For example, researchers have found the specific rate at which mutations happen. When a cell divides, the DNA ladder splits into two half ladders, one for each cell. Each half ladder then becomes the model for replicating the full DNA ladder in each cell. But the replication isn't perfect. It's like a really good typist who makes a mistake every one hundred millionth letter. In humans, that means that in every generation we're packing about sixty mutations.[74]

Most of those mutations don't make that much difference, though, because they occur in parts of the chromosomes that are inactive. Some are even favorable to us, but some are harmful, even lethal. The bad ones—like the mutation that causes cystic fibrosis—are like lightbulbs that have gone out in a big city. They're not easy to find, but when researchers do find them they're on the way to medical breakthroughs.

what Francis Collins calls "the language of God."[72] He playfully says, "GAG means glutamic acid in the language of soil bacteria, the mustard weed, the alligator, and your aunt Gertrude."[73]

The discovery of DNA has led to the field of molecular biology, in which scientists chemically glue together pieces of genetic code in the hope that they can create new treatments to many kinds of diseases. It has also led to the ambitious project of mapping the genomes (or the total amount of genetic information in an organism's chromosomes), from plants to fruit flies to fish to lizards to mice to apes to human beings.

Scientists have learned some striking things by comparing genomes.

GENETICISTS COMPARING HUMANS AT THE DNA LEVEL HAVE DISCOVERED THAT WE ARE 99.9 PERCENT IDENTICAL.

For one, geneticists comparing humans at the DNA level have discovered that we are 99.9 percent identical. That finding includes all the corners of the globe, all races, all human cultures. So it's more than just some cute phrase to say that we're all part of the same human family.[75]

Second, population geneticists (Collins among them) comparing the DNA of racial groups have used mathematical models to reconstruct the geographical movements of humanity. They have concluded that our species has a common ancestor, or set of ancestors, who lived somewhere around 100,000 to 140,000 years ago in Africa. Many scientists assert that this finding synchronizes well with fossil evidence.[76]

Third, geneticists working to compare human and chimpanzee chromosomes have noted that humans have twenty-three chromosomes, chimpanzees twenty-four. If you line them up side by side, they correspond in size and number—with one important exception. It appears that human chromosome #2 is made up of two medium-size chimpanzee chromosomes that, geneticists say, fused into one in some ancient genetic ancestor. Also, if you map the locations of the genes on the chromosomes, pseudogenes (or nonfunctioning genes) on humans appear in the same places as functioning genes on chimpanzees, and vice versa. This poses a sticky question for the traditional view: If humans and chimpanzees were specially, perfectly, precisely created by God, why all the nonfunctioning genes, and why in those parallel locations?[77]

Two creationist rebuttals are:

- *God was following a common pattern when he specially created the two species.*

- *The disabled genes* aren't *non-functioning; we just don't know enough about the functions yet.*

Fourth, pressing back even further in life's ancestry, using computers to track and compare the vast genome data, researchers have found that some human genes match, or closely match, those of other mammals. In addition, many human genes have similar—though not perfect—matches to fish, fruit flies, round worms, yeast, and bacteria. Furthermore, between active genes are long stretches of inactive DNA (often called junk DNA); in these patches the chances of finding genetic matches between humans and nonhumans decreases drastically. (Random mutations in nonfunctioning genes would both increase over time and wouldn't harm reproduction.) The implication in this science, drawn by computer modeling, is that all of life is part of a single evolutionary tree, and that, biologically, humans are part of that tree.[78] This conclusion has been obtained independently of the fossil record, yet, many scientists will argue, lines up with it.

DOES EVOLUTION'S REVOLUTION MEAN THE DEVOLUTION OF FAITH?

The Copernican revolution sought to find the laws of nature to describe what we see in the inanimate world. Darwin brought the Copernican revolution to biology.

Darwin's evolutionary theory appeared to strike a frontal attack at Christianity's self-understanding. The Bible portrays God as a wise and benevolent creator; evolution seemed to portray nature as uncaring, even cruel.

On a more personal level, before he left for his trip on the *Beagle*, Darwin was a believer, convinced by Paley's argument

> DARWIN'S WIFE, EMMA, A DEVOUT CHRISTIAN, WORRIED ABOUT **CHARLES'S SPIRITUAL DESTINY,** FEARING THAT THEY MIGHT BE SEPARATED FOREVER.

for God from design. He had intended, upon his return to England, to take up the simple life of a country preacher. Later in life, having come up with a way of accounting for the diversity of life by naturalistic means alone, he described himself as an unbeliever.

Yet spiritually and emotionally, he was torn, as this excerpt from a letter to his good friend Joseph Hooker shows:

What a book a Devil's chaplain might write on the clumsy, wasteful, blundering, low & horridly cruel works of Nature. My God, how I long for my stomach's sake to wash my hands of it.[79]

Darwin's wife, Emma, a devout Christian, worried about Charles's spiritual destiny, fearing that they might be separated forever. On this, Darwin wrote, "When I am dead, know that many times I have kissed & cryed over this."[80] As a man made in the image of God, Darwin couldn't seem to find a way to overcome the apparent incompatibility.

Let's leave the final word for this chapter to Francis Collins, in his book *The Language of God*:

At this point, godless materialists might be cheering. If humans evolved strictly by mutation and natural selection, who needs God to explain us? To this, I reply: I do. The comparison of chimp and human sequences, interesting as it is, does not tell us what it means to be human. In my view, DNA sequence alone, even if accompanied by a vast trove of data on biological function, will never explain certain special human attributes, such as knowledge of the Moral Law and the universal search for God. Freeing God from the burden of special acts of creation does not remove Him as the source of the things that make humanity special, and of the universe itself. It merely shows us something of how He operates.[81]

07 A SERIOUS APE

A serious ape whom none take seriously,
Obliged in this fool's world to earn his nuts
By hard buffoonery.
—GEORGE (MARION EVANS CROSS) ELIOT (1819–1880),
THE SPANISH GYPSY

George Eliot's "serious ape" was actually a performing monkey named Annibal who'd pass the hat after a juggler did his tricks. A few years ago at a circus on a street corner in New York, I had a similar experience with an organ grinder's monkey. This one took a hat around the circle of people that had gathered and practically demanded that you put something in it. If you wavered, he'd paw at you and even try to put his hand in your pocket. Now that little guy was insistent!

The challenge of Darwinian evolutionary theory is like that. It keeps pawing at us: What is our understanding of science? What is our understanding of faith and the Bible? How should the Bible be interpreted? What is the proper relationship between science and religion? And last: How should we read Genesis 1?

KINGDOM KONG AND KINGDOM COME: DIFFERENCES

This might be too basic, but science and religion are like two kingdoms, which we'll call Kingdom Kong and Kingdom Come. We might say the two are contrasting ways of learning, knowing, applying. They have different scopes of study, limits, methods of gaining knowledge, and languages of discourse.

Different Scopes of Study

Kingdom Kong is all about understanding the natural world: its physical composition, its motions, its laws. It's interested in the visible, temporal, phenomenal world we experience every day. It deals with observable, measurable things in a closed system of cause and effect. This realm is available to our five senses and their extensions through scientific instruments.

Kingdom Come is about trying to see all of reality as God wants us to see. The Bible is dualistic in the sense that it is interested in both the supernatural and the natural. Rather, because God is creator of *everything*, the biblical worldview is very interested both in this world and the next, the seen and the unseen, the temporal and the eternal, the natural and the supernatural. God wants us to come to know him supernaturally through Christ and the Holy Spirit, and then every day to apply his truth in the physical world as we know it. Yes, heavenly rewards are part of the package, but we're not supposed to become so heavenly minded that we're no earthly good.

Different Limits

When you go to a natural history museum, the operative word in the sign is *natural*, not *supernatural*. As Kingdom Kong advances human knowledge, it tends to weed out superstition, magical thinking, and false perceptions. For some scientists—but by no means all—this means weeding out all of religion as well. However, science itself can only look for the *what* and the *how*; it has no authority at all to speak to the supernatural *who* or *why* behind the *what* and the *how*. Even when science tries to quantify or measure the effects of the supernatural, such as in studies on the paranormal or prayers for the sick, it can only get at the supernatural through indirect means: testimonies, self-reporting, that sort of thing. You can't bottle up God, measure him, or put him in a test tube. Sorry, it just doesn't work that way.

> YES, HEAVENLY REWARDS ARE PART OF THE PACKAGE, BUT WE'RE NOT SUPPOSED TO BECOME SO HEAVENLY MINDED THAT WE'RE NO EARTHLY GOOD.

Kingdom Come lays a claim to absolute truth in the supernatural realm, beginning with the crucial truth that God is the creator of the heavens and the earth. It also claims that God has acted in concrete history through the long history of the nation of Israel, the prophets, the coming of Christ, and the birth of the church.

Many Christians also try to say that science proves the Bible or say that the Bible is a valid source of scientific information. However, whether it's proper to say that the Bible intends to give us scientific information is debatable. The Bible comes to us in 2,000- to 3,000-year-old clothing, from wise people who were inspired by God, who knew a lot about human nature, and who knew God, but who simply weren't acquainted with modern science. It could be argued: Why should we feel the need to reach back across the centuries and impose today's science on the Bible?

Different Methods of Gaining Knowledge

Kingdom Kong is an agreed-upon method for gaining increasing knowledge about the natural world. The cycle goes something like this:

- *Hunch (hypothesis)*
- *Test (conduct experiment, measure results)*
- *Revise hunch (based upon the experimental results)*
- *Test again*

> RESEARCHERS IN DIFFERENT PARTS OF THE GLOBE SHOULD BE ABLE TO DUPLICATE THE EXPERIMENT AND GET THE SAME RESULTS. OF COURSE, **RIVALRIES HAPPEN, PERSONALITIES GET INVOLVED, AND SOME PEOPLE FUDGE THEIR NUMBERS.**

It's a hands-on, trial-and-error, never-finished process. The idea of the scientific method is to arrive with confidence at conclusions. Using the scientific method, researchers in different parts of the globe should be able to duplicate the experiment and get the same results. Of course, rivalries happen, personalities get involved, and some people fudge their numbers. But the scientific method also includes built-in correctives like double-blind studies and peer review. In the long run, if you're dishonest in science your dishonesty is going to come back and bite you. The scientific method uses practical reasoning to force out bad ideas and theories and reward ones that work. As a never-finished process, it's constantly correcting itself; scientific revolutions unceremoniously turn widely believed theories on their heads.

The scientific method, then, does not presume to know ahead of time what the results of an experiment will be. The experiment must be done, the results tabulated and compared with others. Any theory worth its salt must be verified with measurable results.

The point here is that genuine science is based upon *methodological* naturalism; it is not a commitment to *philosophical* naturalism. Mainstream science defines itself as methodologically naturalistic. Therefore it has no foothold to say

METHODOLOGICAL NATURALISM: The scientific method, which makes the assumption that observable effects in nature are explainable only by natural causes.

PHILOSOPHICAL NATURALISM: The worldview that claims the natural, physical world is the only real world. It denies the existence of the supernatural; by definition, it is atheistic.

"There's no God!" or "There is a God!" It has chosen to focus only on the physical, material side of things.

On the other hand, *philosophical* naturalism is a worldview that assumes by faith, without any proof whatsoever, that this physical world is the only real world. As such, philosophical naturalism is totally unscientific in its claim that God doesn't exist.

Methodological naturalism (science itself) is a good thing, but philosophical naturalism is a total denial of the biblical worldview and God's truth. But beware! Philosophical naturalism sometimes comes in the guise of science.

Kingdom Come's method for arriving at valid knowledge is different. The core issue is faith. God the Father draws us to himself (John 6:44); God the Son loves us and proves the full measure of his love by dying for us (Romans 5:8); and the Holy Spirit shows us our spiritual need (John 16:8-11), causes us to be born again (Titus 3:5), and helps us grow spiritually (Romans 8:2-6). The objective is not amassing facts in our minds, but getting to know God as Lord and as a personal friend.

> PHILOSOPHICAL NATURALISM IS TOTALLY UNSCIENTIFIC IN ITS CLAIM THAT GOD DOESN'T EXIST.

Knowledge of God depends in part on testimony, in part on finding out God is real in our own experience. The testimony comes from the Bible, God's Word; through others who know Christ (both through history and people we ourselves know); through the teaching and preaching of the gospel; and

INTELLIGENT DESIGN AND SCIENCE: Let's digress for a moment. I'd like to note that the Intelligent Design movement would hotly contest this definition of methodological naturalism as the basis of good science. ID proponents would argue that it's arbitrary for science to completely leave out the supernatural and is an invalid methodology. In other words, ID's whole approach is based on the premise that science *scientifically* demonstrates both a supernatural intelligence *and* design.

On the other side of the coin, it should also be noted that Intelligent Design's definition of science has not been accepted in the mainstream scientific community (including many working Christians who are scientists), which calls ID a philosophy or religion, but not science. I'm not sure how to work around all the technicalities of this problem or how to reconcile the two ideas. But I did want to share this part of the controversy at this point.

through the Holy Spirit speaking through God's Word and directly in our spirits. The Bible serves as our base of authority; no spiritual voice coming from God will contradict God's truth.

In science, theories may come and theories may go, but core assumptions can always be modified by new facts. In matters of faith, some things never change: our *perceptions* of God might change, but God himself doesn't change, Jesus doesn't change (see Hebrews 13:8), and the gospel (or the good news of Jesus Christ) doesn't change.

In our own experience, we can also come to know God's reality through answered prayer and signs and wonders that give glory to Jesus. It's not all about what's going on between our ears; it's not all just words. The apostle Paul said,

> My message and my preaching were not with wise and persuasive words, but with a demonstration of the Spirit's power, so that your faith might not rest on men's wisdom, but on God's power. (1 Corinthians 2:4, 5)

Different Languages of Discourse

All language is symbolic in the sense that we use it to refer to things (material, moral, or spiritual). In Kingdom Kong, the languages of discourse are plain and grounded in things that have, say, a certain molecular weight, or positions in three-dimensional space. It also contains a lot of mathematics. Poetry and history might be used, but only to illustrate points. The main thing is to use language to talk about what is evidentially, measurably there.

In Kingdom Come, a variety of discourses are used as well, each according to the author's needs at the moment. Each way of speaking has a different set of conventions it goes by for bringing home the intended meanings.

It's not possible to talk about God without using metaphors. Calling God "our rock" or "our fortress" is to use a metaphor to make a point. Calling God "good" also forces us to think of something in our experience that is good and then apply that idea to God. It's different from $2+2=4$. But this doesn't mean that language is incapable of bringing home truth. Jesus is The Word—in Greek the expression is the *Logos* of God (John 1:1-3)—who perfectly expresses God's will to us. So we believe God uses human language to convey his truth to us, however imperfectly we may come to understand it.

> **LOGOS:** In Greek philosophy, the grounding rationale principle of the universe. In Christian theology, divine wisdom made manifest in the creation, government, and redemption of the world—and most often associated with the second person of the Trinity, the Son (Jesus).

KINGDOM KONG AND KINGDOM COME: A TRICKY RELATIONSHIP

The first thing to say about the relationship between religion and science is that all truth is God's truth. That is, God is true, his Word is true, and whatever is true in nature (and natural science) cannot be in essential conflict with God's truth. However, trying to figure out how to reconcile religion and science and exactly what that relationship should be is extremely tricky. Let's consider several ways people have looked at this uneasy relationship.

The first can be called essential conflict. In this scenario either religion crushes science or science crushes religion. (Kind of like rock-paper-scissors, except with only two options.) Compromise and finding middle ground are pretty much tossed out the window. For example, Henry Morris, author of *Scientific Creationism*, has said:

> There seems to be no possible way to avoid the conclusion that if the Bible and Christianity are true at all, the geologic ages must be rejected altogether.[82]

Dr. John L. Groenlund of the Institute for Creation Research echoes the same sentiment when he says, "If [Darwinian] evolution is true, then the Bible is not true."[83]

> TRYING TO FIGURE OUT HOW TO **RECONCILE RELIGION AND SCIENCE** AND EXACTLY WHAT THAT RELATIONSHIP SHOULD BE IS EXTREMELY TRICKY.

An opinion from the opposite worldview can be found in T. H. Huxley and James Sully's article in the 1907 edition of *Encyclopedia Britannica*:

> It is clear that the doctrine of Evolution is directly antagonistic to that of creation. Just as the biological doctrine of the transmutation of species is opposed to that of special creation, so the idea of evolution as applied to the formation of the world as a whole is opposed to that of [creation by the will of a creator].[84]

So we see that, even though they come from opposite worldviews, they strongly agree on something! We might go even further and say that those holding these polar views hold the same assumptions about what the Bible and science say. Both assume that science contradicts what the Bible teaches. In America, this viewpoint has been pushed by Christians, agnostics, and anti-Godders. They've sold it, and sold it hard, that you must take Genesis as a literal account, and that that's the only possible way to read the Bible's opening book. An unintended and sad consequence is that, on this one issue, many people end up losing their faith. Another is that a lot of smart Christian students abandon the sciences for fear that what they might learn will conflict with their faith. But rather than abandoning the field, Christians should go into the sciences just like every other field and try to make a difference for Christ.

The second can be termed grudging acceptance. The perspective here is that for all practical purposes either religion or science holds the winning cards, but we'll be nice and allow the other side to have a few minor victories.

The third position is called forced harmonization in the guise of reconciliation. In this view, either the Bible must be harmonized with science or science must be harmonized with the Bible. This perspective often makes statements about how the Bible is God's Word because it is "scientifically correct" on this or that point, such as being the first to tell of the Big Bang theory. Other examples are often brought forth, such as these from the www.christiananswers.net Web site: "roundness of the earth (Isaiah 40:22); almost infinite extent of the . . . universe (Isaiah 55:9); law of conservation of mass and energy (2 Peter 3:7); hydrologic cycle (Ecclesiastes 1:7); vast number of stars (Jeremiah 33:22); law of increasing entropy (Psalm 102:25-27); paramount importance of blood in life processes (Leviticus 17:11); atmospheric circulation (Ecclesiastes 1:6); gravitational field (Job 26:7); and many others."[85] But some argue that, in many cases, it really seems like they're straining and stretching to put words in the mouths of the biblical writers.

> THE PERSPECTIVE HERE IS THAT YOU SHOULDN'T EVEN TRY TO RECONCILE SCIENCE AND RELIGION BECAUSE THEY OCCUPY SUCH DIFFERENT, NON-OVERLAPPING FIELDS OF KNOWLEDGE.

The fourth way to look at the issue is something called non-overlapping magisteria, a phrase coined by evolutionary biologist Stephen Jay Gould to explain his view that "science and religion are not in conflict because their teachings occupy different domains."[86] The perspective here is that you shouldn't even try to reconcile science and religion because they occupy such different, non-overlapping fields of knowledge.

Gould was a Harvard professor and one of America's most famous scientists of the twentieth century (he died in 2002). He used the religious term *magisteria*—with its roots in the Roman Catholic Church, it basically means church leaders holding the power to teach "true doctrine," through divine guidance—to refer to authority in both religion and science. Religion has no authority at all to make judgments in scientific matters or predetermine scientific answers, he argued; but similarly, under this definition, science has absolutely no authority to predetermine or make judgments in religious matters.

Evaluating Gould's position, one good thing about it is that it reduces the conflicts between Kingdom Kong and Kingdom Come. Science, exclusively interested in the natural, can only deal with what *is*; it has absolutely nothing to say about God or meaning or purpose to life or what *should be*.

However, I see a problem with an absolute division between science and the Bible. It's true that religion's focus is the spiritual side of things: God as the *who* of creation, the purpose and meaning to life, and how morality should play out in our lives. However, Christian faith is not intended to serve only as something spiritual with no connection to our present physical reality. God wants us to live out our faith in the real, material world of time and space. Christian faith must, at least in some ways, overlap into the *what* category. And as someone who believes in the authority of God's Word over all of life, it makes me nervous to totally turn over everything in this life to methodological naturalism.

GETTING OUR HEADS INTO THE OLD WORLD

Whatever position we may take on Kingdom Kong and Kingdom Come, we ought to try to let Genesis 1 speak to us as if we were there when it was first told. The first thing we need to realize is that the opening chapters of the Bible were written into a particular historical, cultural, and religious setting—that of ancient Near Eastern pagan polytheism. God pulled the Hebrew people out of this culture, but they were constantly tempted to return to it. If we can have empathy with their situation in life, we can better respect the intent of the author and more fully honor the Bible as God's Word.

To get ourselves prepared mentally, let's imagine that it's 3,500 years ago and that a drama team from the temple in a nearby pagan city has come to present the story of our origins. For the following script, I've pulled together elements from several ancient Near Eastern myths about how the universe came to be, and then taken liberties with the stories themselves to achieve a certain dramatic (and/or comedic) effect.

It's intended to give you a picture of what it might have been like to believe as pagans did back then. It's not a factual representation of real events; it's a fictional story of mythical events.

AN ANCIENT NEAR EAST COSMOLOGY MYTH SKIT

Act 1 Scene 1: "The Deep"	NARRATOR	PLAYERS
	Before there was anything else, there was only "the Deep," a primal ocean of restless, swirling, formless Chaos. Everything to come was contained in her . . .	Four players holding each corner of a sheet, representing the ancient goddess Chaos, gently wave the sheet chest high. Sun god crouches behind, waiting to emerge.
	After eons of time, the sun god emerged by his own sheer willpower from the ancient sea.	The four players slowly lower sheet to shin level to reveal . . .
	He looked around for a dry place to stand on, but as far as he could see—it was wet! Taking some of the watery chaos into his hands, he squeezed it and squeezed it until he created a dry hill. Later an awesome temple there would be dedicated to honor . . . him!	Sun god pantomimes actions described and . . .
	Now, the sun god was alone and lonely.	. . . finishes by polishing his fingernails. *(Chaos/water/sheet actors exit to stage right.)*
	He wanted to create more gods— but he had no mate.	
	Not to fear: This bisexual god, the Great He-She . . . mated with his own shadow!	Sun god pantomimes loneliness. Audience: "Ahh, too bad!"

Act 1 Scene 1: "The Deep" (continued)	Then he gave birth to many gods, some by spitting them out . . .	Wipes brow. Hawks a big loogie.
	. . . and some by vomiting them out of his mouth.	Ralphs violently.
Act 1 Scene 2: "A Terrible Racket"	But after a while, the sun god couldn't get any sleep because of the NOISE and CHAOS his children and grandchildren gods were making.	Insomniac sun god paces back and forth. "Chaos children" play and fight.
	NOTHING he could think of would shut them up.	Sun god: "Will you please just *shut up!*"
	The sun god decided he'd kill all the younger gods. Then he'd be able to get some peace and quiet!	Draws his finger across his throat, then withdraws angrily.
	But when the goddess of primeval Chaos, their "mother," heard of his plan, she would have none of it!	Chaos children shake right index fingers disapprovingly at sun god and say, "No, no, no!"
	Meanwhile, one of the younger gods learned magic . . .	Younger god: pulls rabbit out of hat . . .
	. . . and gained magnificent powers.	. . . and flexes muscles.
	He became a champion, stronger than all the other gods.	*(Meanwhile, 3-person team forms the Chaos dragon, sheet wrapped around them.)*
	This warrior god put on his helmet and rose up against the goddess Chaos, who had transformed herself into a fierce dragon, with a menacing tail and a soul-shuddering roar.	3-person Chaos dragon acts menacing, wags tail, and all three growl a big "grrrrr."
	A terrible battle followed.	
	The warrior god fought against Chaos . . . and in mortal combat vanquished her.	Pantomime battle.

Act 1 Scene 2: "A Terrible Racket" (continued)	(To dragon:) Die, dragon, die.	Younger god mimes spearing Chaos.
	He split her body in two. One half became the sky; the other half became the earth.	Dragon cries out and dies melodramatically.
	He smashed her skull, and out of her eyes flowed the great rivers.	To "split in two": two hold up sheet for the sky, one falls to the ground.
	After all the gore, the sun god's bloodlust was satisfied.	Warrior god takes victor's stance over body.
	He decided NOT to kill the younger gods.	Sun god reappears, pats the heads of the younger gods who have gathered round.
	Eventually there were hundreds of gods responsible for things like mountains, rivers, trees, bread making, beer-brewing, pottery-throwing, and iron-smelting. And for awhile they were a big happy family ("Come on people now . . .") . . . BUT . . . not for long.	He acts grandfatherly and proud. Sun god and younger gods sing, "Come on people now . . . try to love one another right now." (Alternate: "We are family . . .")
Act 1 Scene 3: "Easy Street"	You see, the gods and goddesses actually had to work the land with their own hands for their food. They had to till the fields, plant the crops, dig the water channels, and clear the channels of reeds. As anyone who has ever worked on a farm knows, it was hot, dirty, exhausting work.	Pantomime working in the fields, tilling, planting, digging, pulling out reeds. One says: "This is hot, dirty, exhausting work."
	This got old pretty quick. The gods and goddesses figured they had to do something to lighten their oppressive workload.	Mime throwing down tools and getting together in a huddle.

Act 1 Scene 3:	The wisest and cleverest god among them said, "Hey, let's create humans to work the land so we won't have to! Then we can kick back and relax."	British parliament-style "yeah-yeah"-ing.
"Easy Street" (continued)		
	The gods and goddesses thought this was a good plan. So the wise and clever god got some river clay and made some clay humans.	
	He breathed into the models and they came alive.	Wise and clever god mimes making humans.
	But he strictly limited how long they would live—only the gods and goddesses would live forever.	Blows on them.
	Immediately, the gods put the humans to forced labor.	Like a schoolteacher, he shakes a finger at imaginary humans.
	So the humans dug the channels, tilled the soil, and planted the crops. Every day they provided the gods and goddesses with food and drink.	They mime giving orders.
	The gods and goddesses were happy . . . but not for long . . . I guess they had too much time on their hands . . .	They kick back in chairs, feet up, heads resting in hands. Mime eating grapes, drinking from cups, burping.

A CALL TO WORSHIP

In high contrast, what Genesis 1 is intended to be is a call to us to worship the one true God, the creator of the universe. This is true for Christians and seekers no matter what interpretation of Genesis we have. Also, no matter what interpretation of Genesis makes the most sense to us, we should at least attempt to do three things: let the Scriptures speak for themselves; leave some room for the development of our understanding of both God and science; and leave some room for awe and mystery in our appreciation of God.

To close this chapter, here are a few questions we can think about:

- *Whatever the arguments for or against a literal Genesis, shouldn't God receive the same amount of worship and praise whether it took him a long time to do something, or a short time?*

- *Whatever the arguments for or against geologic time, is it possible to hold to the biblical worldview (God as creator, God as involved in his creation, God loving us) and also a deep-time perspective?*

- *Does our faith need to be threatened by the idea of an old Earth or Big Bang that started (perhaps) about 15 billion years ago?*

- *Can your faith be just as strong if you choose to reject that scientific view?*

- *What are the dangers in wedding any particular scientific theory with Christian faith?*

- *In your opinion, does the biblical worldview and the best that science currently has to offer necessarily need to contradict?*

08 SURRENDERMONKEYS

Theism as a way of defining God is dead.
So most theological God-talk is today meaningless.
A new way to speak of God must be found . . .
***
Since God can no longer be conceived in theistic terms,
it becomes nonsensical to seek to understand Jesus
as the incarnation of the theistic deity.
So the Christology of the ages is bankrupt.
—BISHOP JOHN SELBY SPONG, IN THE ARTICLE
"A CALL FOR A NEW REFORMATION" (1998)

THEISM: The term can be defined as either belief in one God as the creator and ruler of the universe or belief in the existence of a god or gods. (It's important that this is not confused with *deism*, defined at the start of chapter 1, which allows for a creator-God, but states that he has since detached himself from world affairs.)

John Selby Spong, retired Episcopal bishop of Newark, New Jersey, is a surrender monkey. His "Call for a New Reformation" is really a call to wave the white flag, throw in the towel, and give up on the God revealed in both Jewish and Christian history. We need, he says, a new language for God because "most theological God-talk is meaningless."[87]

Obviously, the good bishop is excluding his own God-talk from the meaningless category. He apparently wants us to take *his* God-talk as a beacon shining in the wilderness of Christian darkness.

I'm constantly amazed that a bishop, who took vows to uphold the peace and purity of the church and to proclaim the gospel, could spread such blasphemy and contempt for Christian faith's core beliefs and not receive some kind of censure or discipline. But there he is today, an ex-bishop in good standing, drawing his pension from a church he's tried his best to destroy.

I'd go easier on Spong if he'd had a faith crisis, realized he could no longer affirm the basic biblical worldview and teaching, and then had the honesty and integrity to step down from his position of leadership. But that's not what he did. Instead, he went on the warpath against anything that smells like traditional Christian faith, and he's tried to take his whole church down his revisionist road. Christians who disagree with him he attacks as "fundamentalists," and in his worldview, that's about the worst insult you can utter. In my opinion, Spong ironically exhibits many of the worst attitudes he decries in others:

> IN MY OPINION, SPONG IRONICALLY EXHIBITS MANY OF THE **WORST ATTITUDES** HE DECRIES IN OTHERS: **NARROW-MINDEDNESS, BIGOTRY, AND BELLIGERENCE.**

narrow-mindedness, bigotry, and belligerence. He's a first-rate fundamentalist for his own worldview.

So what is Spong's worldview? It starts by attacking the biblical worldview with arguments from naturalistic science and naturalistic evolution. Then it morphs into religious perspectives that deny the God of the Bible, Christ, and salvation. The danger is clear: Surrendering to the God-denying worldview of naturalism—even though it might seem to be forsaking the spiritual—can open people up to deep spiritual deception.

THE GRINCHES WHO STOLE CHRISTMAS

Bishop Spong is not alone among people who want to remake Christianity into the image of other religions or worldviews. In some Protestant denominations, a significant number of clergy, seminary professors, and lay leaders might not be so in-your-face about it, but they believe the same way Spong does. For them, Spong is a courageous hero. These so-called Christian leaders believe we need to completely reconfigure the core of Christian faith, to turn our backs on: the biblical worldview; God as an all-powerful and loving, personal God; and the core gospel itself. Why would they think this way? Spong gives us a big clue when he says:[88]

> SPONG THINKS THAT JESUS' TEACHING ABOUT A HEAVENLY FATHER IS "HUMANLY DEFINED." SPONG'S GOD IS INCAPABLE OF CARING FOR HUMANITY.

The need for a new theological reformation began when Copernicus and Galileo removed this planet from its previous supposed location at the center of the universe, where human life was thought to bask under the constant attention of a humanly defined parental deity.

Notice how Spong so easily goes on the attack. Spong thinks that Jesus' teaching about a heavenly Father is "humanly defined." Spong's god[xiii] is incapable of caring for humanity.

A few lines later he gives us his next big clue:

[xiii] The lower-case *g* is intentional because Spong's god is entirely a god of his own making.

After [Newton's discovery of mathematically fixed laws of motions of the planets], the Church found itself in a world in which the concepts of magic, miracle, and divine intervention as explanations of anything, could no longer be offered with intellectual integrity.

So for Spong, just because some smart guy figured out some physical laws, miracles are now suddenly impossible and a God who cares for humanity can no longer intervene anywhere. A breathtaking leap of logic. And more:

Next came Charles Darwin who . . . confronted the human consciousness with concepts diametrically opposed to the traditional Christian world view. The Bible began with the assumption that God had created a finished and perfect world from which human beings had fallen away in an act of cosmic rebellion. Original sin was the reality in which all life was presumed to live. Darwin [offered his theory] instead [of] an unfinished and thus imperfect creation out of which human life was still evolving.

> **ORIGINAL SIN:** In Christian theology, the condition of sinfulness that affects all people; this condition is believed by many to mark all humans from conception. It is traditionally viewed as transmitted (including its guilt and consequent penalties) from Adam's first act of disobedience.

Look at all that Spong is asking us to deny. One of the main points of Genesis 1 is to anchor us in a sense of relationship and friendship with God. Since Spong's whole mode is to be destructive, he can't, or won't, call attention to this.

THIS CALLS FOR CHIMPEACHMENT!

Next, Spong denies sin, the cross, and the atonement.

Human beings did not fall from perfection into sin as the church had taught for centuries. We were evolving, and indeed are still evolving, into higher levels of consciousness.

This language of "higher levels of consciousness" comes out of the modern New Age movement, itself based in pop culture interpretations of Buddhism and Hinduism, not Christian faith.

Spong continues:

> *Thus the basic myth of Christianity that interpreted Jesus as a divine emissary who came to rescue the victims of the fall from the results of their original sin became inoperative. So did the interpretation of the cross of Calvary as the moment of divine sacrifice when the ransom for sin was paid.*

Spong approvingly cites the famed psychiatrist Sigmund Freud; Spong wrote that Freud looked at Christianity as nothing more than "deep-seated infantile neurosis." So the only way to save Christian faith, says Spong, is to throw off "pre-modern" Christianity and become what he calls "post-modern."[89] And job # 1 in that project is to get rid of that very bad idea of a caring God in Heaven.

Need I go any further to demonstrate that Spong is a poser? He's happy to wear the honorific ceremonial dress of the bishop's purple shirt and bear titles like Very Right Reverend, but he is no longer a Christian in any genuine sense.

So why is Spong saying these things? The short answer is, he no longer believes in the biblical worldview or what I've called the white-hot core of Christian faith. We might quibble over whether he is an atheist/materialist (believing that the only reality is the material world); a pantheist (everything as impersonal spirit, or god, or "energy"); or a panentheist (a semi-personal type of pantheism, or the idea that an "Ultimate Gee Whiz" has some aspects of personality or soul). Whichever, there's no argument that Spong's religious assumptions are incompatible with and not even remotely friendly to the gospel of Jesus.

PANTHEISM: A doctrine that equates "God" (more like an impersonal absolute) with the forces and laws of the universe; this impersonal "God" is everything.

PANENTHEISM: "God" is viewed as soul and the animating force of the universe; this view is rooted in pantheism but tries to smuggle in ideas of a personal supreme being.

How do we know? We can think of the following as a brightly lit sign over an old, well-known theater: The Bible says with total clarity that God is all-powerful; we can take this as fact through the evidence of all creation. The Bible says God is personal, a fact we can find in the Trinity, in God's communicating to us through the Word and the Holy Spirit, and in his activity in human history. And the Bible says that God loves us and proved it by sending his Son to die for us on the cross.

POSITIVES AND DIFFICULTIES

We've already introduced the five main viewpoints, or approaches, to creation and evolution. The purpose of this next section—and the next four chapters—is to analyze each more deeply.

My goal is to take a nonpartisan stance as we move through this section and to be as fair-minded as I can be.

People are pleased when you agree with them and can take offense if they perceive you're criticizing or badgering them. Nobody likes it when his viewpoint is pushed aside. So let's take this approach.

On the "positives" side of the scale I'll put an empathetic spin on what each approach is trying to accomplish regarding the white-hot core of Christian faith *and* how well it holds to what are currently accepted scientific principles. On the "difficulties" side I'll list critiques brought against that position's interpretations of the Bible's message and of science *from the perspectives of the other positions.*

It might seem that Spong's views don't fit into any of the five approaches we're discussing in this book. Here's the connection: Whatever Spong's own personal religious convictions are, they're closest to the worldview of naturalism. Here are the positives and difficulties of this view:

Surrender Monkey Positives

- *It seeks to take science seriously.*
- *It seeks to take culture seriously.*
- *It seeks to account for our human limitations.*

NEED I GO ANY FURTHER TO DEMONSTRATE THAT **SPONG** IS A POSER?

- *It recognizes the culture in which the Bible was written.*

- *Some allowance is made for questioning, dissent, and dialogue.*

Surrender Monkey Difficulties

- *It utterly caves on the biblical worldview.*

- *It trashes Scripture, making it just another ancient book.*

- *It accuses fundamentalists of "flat-earth literalism"—a phrase that could be defined as insisting the Bible should be taken so literally, at every word, that the Bible would argue that the earth is flat. And for Spong, fundamentalists are the enemy—anyone who believes in historic orthodox Christian faith, in "mere Christianity" ranging from the Apostles' Creed to C. S. Lewis. To Spong, a fundamentalist is anyone who believes in theistic God, his Son Jesus Christ, the authority of the Bible, and Heaven and Hell. And this would include anyone holding to Young Earth, Old Earth, Intelligent Design, or Trinitarian Theistic Evolution views.*

> THE BIBLE SAYS **GOD IS PERSONAL;** I BELIEVE WE CAN SEE THIS AS A **CERTAINTY THROUGH THE TRINITY.**

- *It presumes that the reader can twist the Bible to say anything he or she wants it to say, rather than seeking to determine the intent of the author and allowing the text to have its say.*

- *It assumes that God simply cannot speak or act in his world.*

- *It mocks traditional pictures of God as king, sovereign, providential, or having any degree of control. This mocking view pushes God into a box and views him as "dictatorial," "coercive," and "static."*

- *It's highly prejudicial against Christian faith. It forces highly dubious meanings on the Bible. It ignores some of the most important scriptural themes.*

- *It scoffs at sin and the need for Christ to die on the cross for us.*

- *In forms less extreme than Spong's, it's still deistic: The view is that "god" is remote and ineffective in what little he, she, or it (let's not be so prejudiced as to use a male pronoun!) can do.*

- It's uncritical of materialism, deism, pantheism, and panentheism.

- It's full of weak and even false arguments, attempting to force illogical choices on us like presuming that science and belief in the God of the Bible just cannot exist together in any way.

- It undermines Christian morals, grounding its view of right and wrong entirely on human thinking and reasoning and rejecting absolutely the idea that God can make moral commands.

POSTSCRIPT ON SURRENDER MONKEYS

In the next four chapters, we'll take a close look at the positives and difficulties of the four Christian worldview positions on creation/evolution. I'll pretty much leave it at that—it's up to all of us to ponder the implications.

But with Surrender Monkeys themselves, I can't just leave it at that. This position pretends to be Christian but in fact is unquestionably antagonistic to genuine Christian faith. It turns people away from Christ as Savior. It denies that God cares for them. Spiritually, it's stale and worthless. Therefore, in this book we're not moving forward with this option.

09 OH, GIVE ME A HOME WHERE THE DINOSAURS ROAM

Adam, Eve, and T. Rex:
Giant roadside dinosaur attractions are used by a new breed of creationists as pulpits
to spread their version of Earth's origins
—FRONT-PAGE HEADLINE, *LOS ANGELES TIMES*

Donald Gennaro [after seeing a brachiosaur, a dinosaur with a massive body and very
long neck]: We're gonna make a fortune with this place.
*****

Dr. Alan Grant [holding a newly hatched dinosaur in his hands]: What species is this?
Henry Wu, Jurassic Park scientist: It's . .. uh, a velociraptor.
Grant [in disbelief]: You bred raptors?
—FROM STEVEN SPIELBERG'S *JURASSIC PARK* (1993)

You just gotta love those dinosaurs. Since the time we were kids, they've exercised a magnetic pull on our imaginations. Their sweet-sounding names alone are captivating: apatosaurus, stegosaurus, tyrannosaurus rex, triceritops, iguanadon, pterodactyl. Whether we encounter them in silly cartoons like *The Flintstones*, tacky prehistoric pit stops in the desert, digitized moving images like those in *Jurassic Park*, or in visits to natural history museums, we can't help but gravitate toward them.

When you get right down to it, who wouldn't want to see a real dinosaur up close and personal, rather than just walking past immobile and dried-out museum skeletons? This might help explain why dinosaurs-and-God roadside attractions have popped up in various places across the country. As the pastor of a nondenominational church that meets next to (and publicizes) one of these attractions in Cabazon, California put it, "There's something in [children's] DNA that knows man walked with these creatures on Earth."[90]

Let's look at the strong points that bolster the view of the Young Earth Creationism camp.

POSITIVES FOR YOUNG EARTH CREATIONISM

The Young Earth view is solidly anchored in the biblical worldview in that it believes in God as creator, that God can communicate to humanity, and that God can act in his world. Young Earth Creationism teaches that God reigns and is in control.

Young Earth believes in the Bible as true and authoritative Scripture. It has a high view of the reliability of the Bible and of the trustworthiness of God's Word. YEC resists all attempts to view Scripture as just another ancient human artifact.

Young Earthers aren't afraid to stand up to bullying from other worldviews. They can sniff out atheism, secular humanism, and atheistic social systems like Marxism and Communism from a mile away.

SECULAR HUMANISM: A set of beliefs, or philosophy, that advocates human values and rejects the supernatural and religion.

Young Earthers preserve a special place for men and women being created in the image of God, fiercely turning away any attempts to reduce humanity to mere animals.

They want to honor the Bible by sticking to its plain, simple, and literal meanings, though young earthers would acknowledge there are plenty of figurative passages in the Bible as well. The attitude is, in something you hear repeated a lot: "God said it, I believe it, that settles it." Thus, faith and trusting God are central to the outlook—human reason shouldn't trump God and faith.

> YOUNG EARTH ALLOWS FOR **NATURAL SELECTION AND MICROEVOLUTION,** OR MODIFICATIONS WITHIN SPECIES.

Young earthers want to have the same attitude toward the Old Testament that they understand Jesus had. Jesus revered God's Word; he said that he did not come to abolish the law but to fulfill it; and he made reference to Jonah and other Old Testament figures and events. In the same way, they argue, we should have the highest respect for God's Word.

Young Earth's position affirming the biblical narrative of creation, fall, and redemption has plenty of precedent within both the Jewish and Christian faith traditions.

Young Earth believes God is an all-knowing and all-powerful creator; in other words, that God is intelligent and that he is a designer. These basic truths line up with the biblical worldview and are things with which all Christians should agree.

Young Earth allows for natural selection and microevolution, or modifications *within* species.

And Young Earth says that we have a moral purpose on earth, that life isn't just about survival. God wants more for us than to merely live by a kill-or-be-killed philosophy.

DIFFICULTIES FOR YOUNG EARTH CREATIONISM

We now turn to difficulties for Young Earth Creationism. Please remember that these difficulties are arguments against YEC from other Christians who share Young Earth's commitment to the white-hot core but don't agree with YEC's interpretations of the Bible, science, or how to bring science and religion together.

"Kinds" as "Species"

Young Earth Creationism (along with Old Earth Creationism) assumes that the word *kinds* in Genesis 1:11, 12, 21, 24, and 25 (the Hebrew word is *miym*[91]) refers or is very close to the modern scientific classification of species. Therefore, they argue, "according to their kinds" means that species may change some, but they cannot change into *other* species.

But theistic evolutionists (and some in the Intelligent Design camp) would point out that nowhere does the Bible define *kinds* or say that kinds or species can't evolve into other species. They would call this "an argument from silence."[92] What God did say to the living creatures in the seas and in the air was, "Be fruitful, and multiply" (Genesis 1:22, *KJV*), a command that potentially allows for lots and lots of multiplication and occasional variations.

Theistic evolutionists would say that if we take *kinds* to mean the broad categories under the biological classification of phylum, then there would be plenty of opportunity for species diversification.[93]

> **PHYLUM:** Primary divisions of a kingdom (animal or plant) that rank next, in size, above a *class*.

"Flat-Earth" Literalism

The other approaches would say that Young Earth saddles itself with both a limited Bible interpretation and bad science.

They would say to Young Earthers: If you want to take those "days" in Genesis purely at face value, as literal days, then to be consistent you also need to buy into other cosmological-type statements found in the Old Testament, such as that the dry land floats between "the waters above" and "the waters below" (Genesis 1:2, 6, 7; Genesis 2:5, 6; Genesis 7:11; Genesis 8:2) and that the earth rests on "pillars" (1 Samuel 2:8, *KJV*; Job 9:6; Psalm 75:3).

They would add that if these statements are taken as cosmological beliefs, or beliefs on the origins and nature of the universe—and similar beliefs are shared by other cultures in the ancient Near East—then they lack good science and are outmoded.

The other approaches would say that Young Earth's method of interpreting Genesis 1—at least in terms of its understanding of "days"—is overly literal and opens the door for inconsistent, illogical thinking.

Replaying Galileo

The other approaches would criticize Young Earth Creationism for having an inadequate understanding of what science is and does. Like the Roman Catholic Church in Galileo's time, YEC can be accused of tying itself to a particular scientific theory. When scientific theories change, as they often do, the movement makes it hard for young earthers to adjust, their opponents argue.

Opponents would say that Young Earth's arguments for why "scientific creationism" must be true come almost entirely from the Bible, religion, philosophy, and probabilities based upon assumptions, but not from experimental evidence. As such, the opponents argue, YEC cannot be considered as science because the methods used do not follow the scientific method and the outcomes of the research are predetermined.

Young earth creationists also are criticized for assuming that macroevolution and the worldview of naturalism absolutely go together; they make no effective distinction between the naturalistic methodology upon which science is based and the philosophical worldview of naturalism that some (but by no means all) scientists have.

Extra Hoops to Jump Through for Conversion

From an evangelistic viewpoint, approaches that improperly plant anti-evolutionism in the white-hot core of Christian faith can hinder people from coming to Christ. In other words, Young Earth (and to a lesser extent, Old Earth Creationism and Intelligent Design) can be accused of giving people the impression that they must jump through the anti-evolution hoop before they become believers (or, at least, "full believers"). I'm aware or have read of cases where some have been excluded from leadership or fellowship if they do not share their larger faith community's literalist interpretation. In effect, YEC could be accused of saying to non-Christians and Christians alike, "If you aren't anti-evolution, you can't be in the in-group, you're in the out-group, and you're in grave error. If (somehow) you are saved, it's only by God's grace and the skin of your teeth."

Missing the Main Thing in Genesis 1

From the perspective of historic and biblical theology, Young Earth's focus on anti-Darwinism and anti-evolution (along with Old Earth and Intelligent Design) can be accused of taking people's eyes off the prize in Genesis 1. The main goal of the Bible's opening chapter is to overturn polytheism (many gods), to get people to worship the one true creator-God, and to see all people as created in God's image.

Relying on Pseudoscience

Some of Young Earth's scientific claims have led those in other camps to suggest that YEC's ventures into providing positive, empirical evidence for its viewpoint have led to errors and embarrassment.

Theistic evolutionists and some in the Intelligent Design and Old Earth Creationism camps would say that Young Earth's worldwide flood could not have produced the rocks or fossil record, nor the oil and coal reserves, nor the chalk layers, nor the Grand Canyon. However, others within Old Earth and ID do hold to a worldwide flood. Others question a worldwide flood interpretation on the basis of internal evidence: Animals leaving the ark would have had nothing to eat if all the earth's vegetation had been destroyed by the flood; the distribution

> THERE ARE THOSE WITHIN THE THEISTIC EVOLUTION, INTELLIGENT DESIGN, AND EVEN OLD EARTH CREATIONISM CAMPS WHO SAY THAT **YOUNG EARTH'S WORLDWIDE FLOOD COULD NOT HAVE PRODUCED THE ROCKS OR FOSSIL RECORD.**

of kangaroos, koalas, and animals in other isolated habitats argues against a general fanning out of animals from the ark; thousands of feet of sedimentary rock are found below the major dinosaur boneyards.

John Whitcomb's book *The Genesis Flood* (1961) and Stanley Taylor's film *Footprints in Stone* (1972) touted supposedly comingled human and dinosaur tracks in Glen Rose, Texas. They presumed they had evidence that they really didn't have, and when the scientific evidence came in, they had to back away from their claims.[94] Today, hardly any young earthers push the Glen Rose footprints, but they still argue for human-dinosaur coexistence.[95]

Lame Nay-Saying

Young Earth's counterarguments for why evolution can't be true or can't happen are weak, other viewpoints might argue. The claims that evolution is "just a theory" or that it's "just a faith position" ignores how many scientific disciplines independently support the theory. The contentions that the fossil evidence is nonexistent; or that "Gish's Fish" (Duane Gish compared a fish skeleton with those of animals to show how dissimilar they are[96]) is different from birds or mammals—these assertions don't take into account what the fossil record does show, scientists say. And Christians who accept Theistic Evolution refute YEC claims that we can't see evolution happening today—TE commonly points to how viruses like HIV are constantly mutating.

Death and Disease Before the Fall

Young Earthers claim that the original creation was perfect ("very good," in Genesis 1:31), and therefore no death or disease yet plagued the earth; these things came only after the fall of man.

However, Old Earth, Intelligent Design, and Theistic Evolution would point out that the fossil record contradicts this scenario. And those outside the Young Earth camp would make the case that "very good" does not necessarily mean "no death or disease"; a thriving, renewing ecological system could certainly be included in the definition of "very good."

Also, the Bible doesn't say death didn't occur among animals before the fall (it's silent on this point). Therefore, many of Young Earth's opponents would regard this YEC position as reading into the text.

Opposing views also would say that if Young Earth Creationism is true, then all fossils had to be deposited *after* the fall. However, this position is not supported by the rock record, many scientists will say.

No Fossil Rabbits in the Precambrian

Young Earth Creationism often offers as evidence the explosion of life forms in the Cambrian as evidence for God creating all the species within a single week. (Old Earth and Intelligent Design proponents also look at the Cambrian explosion as possible evidence for God being especially creative in producing life forms at that time.)

> **CAMBRIAN:** The geologic period defined by scientists in which there was a sudden appearance of hard-body fossils, beyond multi-cellular organisms like sponges; these finds lead to the frequently referenced "Cambrian explosion." The era is placed by scientists at between 542 million and 488 million years ago.

However, according to geologic time—which is accepted by Old Earth, Intelligent Design, and Theistic Evolution proponents—the Precambrian era lasted from about 3.8 billion years ago to about 542 million years ago. In all the rocks of that era, the only fossils of life forms ever found have been very primitive organisms, like bacteria and algae. From that time on, the fossil record records a sequence of advances in diversity and complexity. Someone once asked the famous British biologist J. S. B. Haldane what evidence would falsify Darwinism once and for all. He answered, "Fossil rabbits in the Precambrian."[97] Haldane was saying that finding a fossil rabbit (or crocodile or giraffe or any other vertebrate, for that matter) and verifying the find would completely blow Darwinism out of the water. Claims for such evidence have been made, but no such evidence has ever been authenticated.

Another way of saying this, Youth Earth opponents say, is that if YEC were true, the fossil record would be all jumbled up, since all animals were created at the same time, and because of the great flood. The fossils certainly wouldn't be neatly stacked in a discernible sequence from simpler to more complex. And yet, that's what paleontology shows.

PALEONTOLOGY: A branch of geology that studies life, especially in prehistoric times, through plant and animal fossils.

The "Appearance of Age" Problem

Non-young earthers argue that the claim by some young earth creationists that God made the earth with "the appearance of age" when in actuality it's only 6,000 to 10,000 years old stretches belief. Why would God create a world that appeared to be very old when it wasn't? Also, why would God create the appearance of stars and galaxies outside the 6,000-year light-year bubble if they don't in fact exist? These kinds of explanations seem damaging, YEC opponents say, because they make God into a cosmic trickster and don't do much to boost our confidence in his truthfulness.

Genomes and Junk DNA

Another problem for Young Earth Creationism (along with Old Earth and Intelligent Design) is that molecular biology and recent genome studies do not contradict, but affirm and continue to advance, scientific understanding of evolutionary theory. YEC cannot explain these findings from molecular biology and genome studies that scientists claim allow them to read the history of evolution almost like a book.

Young earth creationists find themselves struggling to adequately explain why the DNA of humans is 95 percent to 98.5 percent identical to chimpanzees, or why God would create humans with long segments of nonfunctioning DNA (sometimes called junk DNA) that are paralleled in chimpanzees.

YEC, Old Earth, and ID anti-evolutionists have responded that this coincidence may be evidence that God was working from similar design patterns.

Evolution as Inherently Antispiritual

Young Earth, like Old Earth and Intelligent Design, is deeply suspicious of and even offended by the evolutionary idea of a single tree of life, of humans and apes having a common ancestor. They're repulsed by the idea of a common descent of all living things because this seems to teach that humans are no longer special and no longer can be thought of as being created in God's image. Young earthers infuse Darwinism with an antispiritual message.

However, Christian theology has always taught that humans are physical/material and soul-inhabited/spiritual beings. Our biology is not the whole story, in other words. So theistic evolutionists, if not some in the ID camp, would argue that it is possible *both* for God to breathe into us the breath of spiritual awareness and for evolution's story of "from goo to you" to be true.

> THEY'RE REPULSED BY THE IDEA OF A COMMON DESCENT OF ALL LIVING THINGS BECAUSE THIS SEEMS TO TEACH THAT **HUMANS ARE NO LONGER SPECIAL** AND NO LONGER CAN BE THOUGHT OF AS BEING CREATED IN GOD'S IMAGE.

A "God of the Gaps" Problem

Opposing viewpoints would say that Young Earth Creationism adheres to a "God of the gaps" mentality, similar to ancient peoples' understanding of God (or the gods, depending on the culture) "doing" everything that couldn't be naturally explained. (Theistic Evolution also brings this criticism against Old Earth and Intelligent Design.) It could be argued that YEC wants to push away naturalistic explanations for things because they seem to take away from God's glory: for each thing that gets explained by natural laws, it would seem that God loses a little bit of his sovereignty. If this keeps happening, it's like putting God out of a job and giving people reasons to think of God as unnecessary.

A theistic evolutionist might respond that God (in all his infinite wisdom) intelligently designed and created nature to be fully gifted and equipped to bring forth life, with all its wonder and diversity. But in this view, young earthers would take a lower view of nature, seeing it as less-than-good, even crippled.[98]

10 STARLIGHT MONKEYS

When I was eight, I started saving to buy a telescope. . . . With my father's help, I designed and built a mount and, at last, peered through the telescope to the heavens above.

I was stunned. I had never seen anything so beautiful, so awesome. The spectacle was too good not to share. . . .

Cosmology is . . . not a subject just for ivory tower academics. Cosmology is for everyone.

—HUGH ROSS, *THE CREATOR AND THE COSMOS: HOW THE GREATEST SCIENTIFIC DISCOVERIES OF THE CENTURY REVEAL GOD* (1993)

If the Big Bang started the whole shebang, as Old Earth Creationism says it did, then there's a good reason we're inexorably drawn to the night sky: if we tilt our necks upward just a little, we're gazing back toward our origins, almost like a baby gazing up at its mother.

But there's more to the universe than just the physical stuff. We look at the night sky and see evidence of God's majestic works. We can't help ourselves. We're driven by two pairs of impulses: those of making observations and those of interpreting them; those of facts drawn from evidence and those of the spiritual. At heart, Old Earth Creationism's quest is to bring these human impulses together into an integrated whole.

When I first started teaching on creation and evolution, I put Young Earth and Old Earth Creationism together in the same category because of the similarities. But as I studied more and talked to people, my "Three Christian Approaches to Evolution" just wasn't working. OEC sees itself as a separate perspective from Young Earth Creationism.

POSITIVES FOR OLD EARTH CREATIONISM

Like Young Earth, Old Earth Creationism is solidly anchored in the biblical worldview. It believes in God as creator and that God can communicate to humanity and act in his world; he reigns and is in control.

It shares a number of views with Young Earth Creationism. Like YEC, Old Earth believes the Bible is true and authoritative Scripture, has a high view of the reliability and trustworthiness of God's Word, and resists all attempts to view Scripture as just another ancient human artifact.

> LIKE YOUNG EARTH, OLD EARTH CREATIONISM IS SOLIDLY ANCHORED IN THE BIBLICAL WORLDVIEW. IT BELIEVES IN **GOD AS CREATOR** AND THAT **GOD CAN COMMUNICATE TO HUMANITY.**

Like Young Earth, Old Earth understands the threat of the materialist philosophy and worldview coming in the form of naturalism, atheism, secular humanism, Marxism, and Communism.

Like Young Earth, Old Earth discerns the difference between the biblical worldview and polytheism, dualism, pantheism, and New Age-ism.

BIBLICAL WORLDVIEW (first discussed in chapter 2): The belief and life-philosophy that God is the creator of the universe and acts freely in the universe; it believes we can come into a relationship with him through his Son, Jesus Christ, and through the Holy Spirit.

NEW AGE: A cultural movement, popularized in the 1980s, concerned with spiritual consciousness and combining various beliefs and practices such as reincarnation, astrology, meditation, holistic medicine, and more.

Like Young Earth, Old Earth teaches that men and women are created in the image of God and cannot be reduced to an animal nature.

Old Earth Creationism wants to honor the Bible but has a different interpretation of the plain, simple, and literal meaning of the texts. Just as with the Young Earth viewpoint, faith and trusting God are central to this outlook. But old earthers become more comfortable with metaphorical language at certain spots in the biblical text.

Old Earth Creationism takes geology, physics, and astronomy seriously.

Old Earth sees no essential conflict between science and religion and desires to fully employ science and bring it into harmony with faith.

Old Earth understands itself to be literally interpreting God's Word, fully respecting its authority and truthfulness.

Like Young Earth Creationism—and to a certain extent Intelligent Design and Theistic Evolution—Old Earth flows with the traditional Christian narrative of a historical fall of man through the choice of sin, of sin passing through the generations, and of atonement and redemption through the death and resurrection of Jesus Christ.

Like the other three biblical worldview positions, Old Earth believes God is an all-knowing and all-powerful creator—an intelligent designer. Old earth creationists simply understand differently from the other approaches *how* God did the intelligent creating.

Like Young Earth and Intelligent Design, Old Earth allows for natural selection and microevolution.

> LIKE YOUNG EARTH AND INTELLIGENT DESIGN, **OLD EARTH ALLOWS FOR NATURAL SELECTION AND MICROEVOLUTION.**

Old Earth highlights the spiritual significance of man's existence on earth. Hugh Ross defines this as "the observation that the universe has all the necessary and narrowly defined characteristics to make human life possible."[99]

Like Young Earth, Intelligent Design, and Theistic Evolution, Old Earth affirms our moral purpose on earth and God's right to determine moral laws and command obedience to them.

HOW OLD EARTH DIFFERENTIATES ITSELF FROM YOUNG EARTH

What follows are some viewpoints that old earthers hold that amount to key differences with young earth creationists.

With regard to the first chapters of Genesis, old earthers have sought to free themselves from the charge that young earthers can face, that the text is read too literally. Old earthers will state that until the deep-time challenges of geology and astronomy, Christians and Jews had little reason to question 24-hour "days" of creation. However, on the strength of the scientific evidence, old earth creationists make the leap to accepting deep time, an earth of about 4.5 billion years, and a universe of about 11 billion more. OEC doesn't feel the need to stay loyal to a pre-nineteenth century view of time. So no one can accuse old earthers of being "flat-earthers" or pre-Copernican in their outlook of astronomy.

DIFFICULTIES FOR OLD EARTH CREATIONISM

Now let's consider some objections that Old Earth Creationism must face from the other Christian approaches in the creation/evolution debate.

A Slippery Slope

From the perspective of Young Earth Creationism, Old Earth Creationism has elevated human reason over God's Word. It is on the slippery slope to naturalism and has badly compromised biblical authority by suggesting that "days" can be eras of millions of years or that the earth is billions of years old. YEC considers its high view of Scripture to be better than OEC's lower view.

"Kinds" as "Species"

Like Young Earth, Old Earth is essentially anti-evolutionistic, basing its opposition on two major assumptions:

- *that the word* kind *in Genesis 1 has the fairly precise scientific meaning of "species"*
- *that Genesis 1 pretty much excludes the possibility of organisms evolving from one species to another.*

Theistic evolutionists would look at Old Earth Creationism and say that OEC wants to be scientific—accepting the rigors of the scientific method with regard to astronomy, geology, and physics—but then, at the same time, resist the findings of the scientific method as applied to the biological sciences, sending a double message.

Where to Draw the Line?

Hermeneutics is the science and art of interpreting texts. It involves carefully considering the cultural and linguistic perspectives of the author(s) of the texts as well as our own.

Old Earth Creationism seeks to free itself from what it sees as Young Earth's strict literalism in Genesis 1, but the OEC approach can create potential problems with how to interpret other passages. The flood narrative of Genesis 6–9 is often used as a ready point of debate: should it be taken literally as a worldwide event, or was it somehow just regional? (Read Genesis 7:20-24, however, and it's hard to picture a "local," as it's sometimes called, or regional flood.) Does the long day in Joshua 10:13 mean the earth stopped spinning on its axis for a few hours, or can we suppose that there might have been other less drastic explanations? Old earthers can disagree even among themselves on how to answer these questions because even within their own camp there is disagreement on which interpreting principles should prevail. The three other

Christian-based positions (Young Earth, Intelligent Design, and Theistic Evolution) might very well object that it's hard to know what interpreting principles are being employed by old earthers and if they're being consistently used. Where do you draw the line? It's not always an easy question.

Squeezing Science into the Bible and Vice Versa

Like Young Earth, Old Earth Creationism can be charged that its arguments for why Darwinian evolution must be false come not from empirical science but from the Bible, philosophy, and statistical probabilities. Is OEC limited in the scientific realm (even with scientists like Hugh Ross among the camp!)? Do its methods require predetermined results? Theistic Evolution and Intelligent Design opponents might answer yes to both.

For example, to some, the old earthers who subscribe to the gap theory are really beginning to sound like they're asking for special pleading. It's hard to imagine that the intent of the text is to teach an immense span of time between Genesis 1:1 and 1:2, the opponents would say. Plus, nothing in the narrative of Genesis chapters 6 through 9 hints at the idea that we need to scissors-and-paste that section into that slot.

Opponents would say that an Old Earth agenda from outside the actual biblical text (that is, an effort to correct the biblical interpretation so that it is compatible with an old earth) is driving the interpretation.

Replaying Galileo

With its emphasis on geology and astronomy, Old Earth Creationism does not exactly reproduce the Galileo problem (of being tied to one particular scientific theory). But like Young Earth, OEC still tends to tie Christian faith to the particular theory of anti-evolutionism; it can be accused of coming very close to making it part of its creed.

Extra Hoops to Jump Through for Conversion

From an evangelistic viewpoint, the nay-saying message of anti-evolutionism in Old Earth (and Young Earth, and Intelligent Design proponents who share it) can become confused with the positive message of the gospel. An evangelistic response might be: Rather than laboring through anti-evolutionary arguments to prove that the Bible is true, wouldn't it make more sense to make sure we have firmly established the overall biblical worldview that God is the creator and that we, who are created by him and for him, have moral accountability to him? That would then let interesting (but second-order) questions of how to integrate science and religion come up later in the discipleship process.

Missing the Main Thing in Genesis 1

A criticism from the perspective of historical theology might go like this: The polytheistic (many gods) systems of the ancient Near East taught that only gods, kings, warriors, and heroes had real value, dignity, and worth. Common people were basically the slaves of the rulers, and women were just slave property. But the gospel (good news) of Genesis 1 for the ancient world was that God loves us and created all people, including common people (men and women), with innate dignity, value, and worth. Shouldn't this be the message from Genesis 1 that Christ-followers should be shouting from the rooftops?

> THEISTIC EVOLUTION WOULD SAY THAT OLD EARTH'S ATTEMPTS TO REFUTE MACROEVOLUTION ARE BASICALLY THE SAME AS YOUNG EARTH'S.

"It's Not Really Science"

Science predicts specified results, is testable, and its hypotheses can be falsified. Science is open-ended because you don't know in advance what the results will be. Intelligent Design or Theistic Evolution opponents may argue that the outcomes of Old Earth research are predetermined because they must lead to anti-evolutionism. Therefore, OEC does not follow the scientific method in its truest sense, they say.

Their opponents would argue that old earth creationists try to harmonize the Bible with existing science, but that Old Earth is not at the forefront of expanding our knowledge of the physical world.

Lame Nay-Saying

Theistic Evolution would say that Old Earth's attempts to refute Darwin's theory are basically the same as Young Earth's (and Intelligent Design, where those in that camp do the same): the lack of transitional fossils from one species to another; entropy (the second law of thermodynamics); evolution as "just a theory"; evolution as "not observable today." But to many in the scientific community, these arguments don't hold water.

Still No Fossil Rabbits in the Precambrian

Many geologists argue that the fossil record is not all mixed up; there's a discernible fossil order from less to more complex organisms over long periods of time. So Old Earth's belief that Darwinian evolution did not happen could be taken to mean that every time a new species arose, God did it apart from genetic mutations, as an independent, special miracle. The question, then, for young earth and old earth creationists—as posed by theistic evolutionists—is this: Why is this special creations scenario so much more compelling than God creating the world, sparking life at some point by miracle or providential means, and then letting evolution kick in and superintending the process as it went on?

SPECIAL CREATION: The origin and diversity of life come from acts of God; each species was separately created. Darwinism is rejected outright.

Massive Die-Offs

Old Earth Creationism allows for fossils to be layered in sediment and for massive extinctions prior to human habitation, unlike Young Earth. But OEC (with most in the Intelligent Design camp) would speculate that God specially designed and created each and every species, only to have massive die-offs.

Theistic evolutionists might respond: "You believe God is all-powerful. Theoretically, God could specially, miraculously create each and every species in a discernible order from less to more complex. But why would God do that?"

Genomes and Junk DNA

Theistic evolutionists argue that because of its commitment to anti-evolutionism, old earthers (like young earthers and most in the Intelligent Design camp) must resist findings from genome studies and molecular biology that point to species-to-species evolution (and common descent.

Evolution as Inherently Antispiritual

Like Young Earth and Intelligent Design, Old Earth assumes that evolution removes the dignity of humanity because of the supposed biological connection to apes and earlier forms of life. But material, physical descent does not have to obliterate our spiritual side, theistic evolutionists would argue.

> LIKE YOUNG EARTH AND INTELLIGENT DESIGN, OLD EARTH ASSUMES THAT **EVOLUTION REMOVES THE DIGNITY OF HUMANITY** BECAUSE OF THE SUPPOSED BIOLOGICAL CONNECTION TO APES AND EARLIER FORMS OF LIFE.

A "God of the Gaps" Problem

Theistic evolutionists would say that, like Young Earth, Old Earth suffers from the "God of the gaps" problem, but perhaps to a lesser extent. The thinking goes that the more science explains away the mysterious gaps (that people previously had attributed to God, or polytheistic gods) with explanations proven by the scientific method, apparently the less God has to do. This mentality (theistic evolutionists would also fault Intelligent Design with it) is seen by those in the TE camp as simply unnecessary.

11 MONKEYWRENCHING

We call our strategy "the wedge." . . . A wedge can eventually split [a solid log] by penetrating a crack and gradually widening the split. In this case the ideology of scientific materialism is the apparently solid log.

—PHILLIP E. JOHNSON, *DEFEATING DARWINISM BY OPENING MINDS* (1997)

While Flanders is on the stand in court, Homer's antics cause him to crack under pressure and he calls Homer an ape, which leads the judge to believe Homer resembles the missing link—putting a monkey wrench in the prosecutors' case . . .

—"THE MONKEY SUIT" EPISODE, *THE SIMPSONS* (2006)

From serious debates to cartoons, monkey wrenching is a time-honored tactic. With a simple flick of the wrist, the one doing the wrenching—literally or figuratively—can wreck entire sets of gears and bring large machines to a grinding halt.

Phillip Johnson's "wedge" is a monkey wrench thrown into the Naturalistic Evolution-and-science worldview machine. Johnson calls a naive, soft accommodation with Darwinism not possible because "scientific materialists genuinely believe that materialism and science are inseparable, that the realm of objective reality belongs entirely to science and that belief in a supernatural Creator is a holdover from the past that has no place in a rational mind."[100]

> **MATERIALISM:** The philosophical doctrine that matter is the only reality and that everything in the world—including mind, thought, will, and feeling—can be explained only by matter and physical phenomena.

Johnson argues that it's unwise for Christians who are serious about their faith to try to win favor with the culture or to try shallow accommodation with evolutionists. The reason, he says, is not that God can't work through evolution, at least to a limited extent. The real problem, he says, is not evolutionary science but that "modern science protects its grand theory of evolution by starting with the basic assumption that God is out of the picture."[101]

We have no way of knowing, but maybe the producers of *The Simpsons* episode mentioned at the start of this chapter were trying to throw their own humorous monkey wrench into the arguments of the creationist-and-intelligent-design machine. And we can laugh at the silliness of *The Simpsons*, but what underlies the silliness is very important.

Intelligent Design began as a faith-based objection to, and rejection of, Darwinism (sharing those same values with Old Earth Creationism and Youth Earth). To this day, Intelligent Design proponents generally consider Darwinism and neo-Darwinism to be failed theories for explaining life's amazing diversity.

However, if you look closer at the debate within the Intelligent Design movement, the spectrum of opinions regarding evolution—especially in the past ten years—can be remarkably broad:

- *Some ID proponents believe that each and every species on the planet, from algae to insects to giraffes to humans, were specially, directly, and miraculously created "just so" by God. In this view, God was very hands-on the whole time.*

- *Some in the ID movement believe that God allowed all the other plant and animal species to evolve over millions of years, but that humans were specially, supernaturally created by him.*

- *Others concentrate on God's direct, supernatural hand in forming irreducibly complex biological systems—like the eye or the bacterial flagellum (those incredible molecular motors-and-tails that allow bacteria to move)—and seemingly leave the question of evolution open.*

- *Other IDers focus their attention on the almost incalculably small probabilities of life coming from nonlife and concluding that God must have directly, miraculously intervened to create life, thus leaving the possibility of macroevolution open.*

- *And last, some IDers push their investigations all the way back to the first billionths of a second of the Big Bang when, they argue, God set the physical constants and parameters like gravity and strong and weak nuclear forces. All of those things would eventually lead to an earth inhabitable by humans who would one day be able to look back on the whole process with hindsight and identify how everything began.*

IN SHORT, SOMETIMES ID CAN LOOK MORE LIKE THEISTIC EVOLUTION AND SOMETIMES MORE LIKE **OLD EARTH CREATIONISM**, DEPENDING ON THE ISSUE AND WHO'S DOING THE ADVOCATING.

In short, sometimes ID can look more like Theistic Evolution (allowing for macroevolution, or modification from one species to another) and sometimes more like Old Earth Creationism (only permitting microevolution, or modification within species), depending on the issue and who's doing the advocating.[102]

But let's go deeper into the positives for and difficulties facing the Intelligent Design movement.

POSITIVES FOR INTELLIGENT DESIGN

More than any of the other approaches, the ID movement emphasizes worldviews. In our pluralistic culture, especially in academia, this is crucial. Intelligent Design leads the way in publicizing the threat to faith and culture that lurks in materialist philosophy and other less-than-biblical and anti-biblical worldviews. There is much to applaud in the ID movement's work in bringing worldview conflicts into the bright light of day.

> **PLURALISM:** The term is applied in many ways—religiously, philosophically, culturally, and scientifically, among others; religiously, it is loosely defined as the acceptance of all religious paths as equally valid.

Intelligent Design takes the position that the Bible does not have to be interpreted literally at every point. (Some in the ID camp might, for instance, interpret the Old Testament stories of Jonah or Job as dramatic plays or literary works of fiction.) Rather, it seeks to critique evolution on its philosophical assumptions and on its science.

The ID movement uses a respected biblical and theological argument, the argument for design; it seeks to show how the diversity and complexity in life demonstrate signs of intelligence and design everywhere.

Intelligent Design, with its focus on God as an all-powerful and intelligent designer, is fully compatible with the biblical worldview.

ID proponents believe the Old and New Testaments of the Bible are true and authoritative Scripture. And ID fully respects Jesus' attitude toward the Old Testament.

Like Young Earth and Old Earth Creationism, ID's resistance to a purely materialistic understanding of humanity preserves the biblical idea that men and women are more than mere animals, and that they are created in the image of God and spiritually wired for a relationship with him.

Intelligent Design accepts the grand narrative of the Bible, which—I was taught long ago in Bible study—is the creation, fall, and redemption of humans. (This narrative stands in stark contrast to naturalism, which says, "No God, no sin, no redemption.")

Like Young Earth and Old Earth, ID affirms our moral purpose on earth and God's right to determine moral laws and command obedience to them.

RESPONSES TO PERCEIVED CREATIONIST PROBLEMS

What follows are some ways Intelligent Design has sought to overcome what it sees as problems in Young Earth and Old Earth Creationism views.

Agreeing with Old Earth, ID rejects what it sees as Young Earth's restrictive literal reading of the "days" in Genesis 1, with both accepting deep time as understood by many geologists and astronomers.

When versions of scientific creationism as presented by young earth and old earth creationists got rebuffed in the courts in the 1980s and 1990s, Intelligent Design stepped up and tried to keep the door open for God in public awareness and in public school science classrooms. ID has achieved a measure of success in the first, but far less acceptance in the second (which we'll look at in chapter 14).

Where Old Earth often uses the arguments from astronomy and physics, Intelligent Design expands the argument to include biology. This includes author and professor William Dembski's research on information theory and the work of Michael Behe (professor and author of *Darwin's Black Box*) on irreducible complexity (see definition, chapter 3).

DIFFICULTIES FOR INTELLIGENT DESIGN

Now let's consider some critiques of the Intelligent Design movement from the other Christian approaches to creation/evolution—Young Earth, Old Earth, and Theistic Evolution.

A Slippery Slope

Young Earth rejects Intelligent Design's acceptance of deep time, which, to young earthers, implies a "low" view of Scripture and heading down a slippery slope that could lead to denying God's Word. Young Earth and Old

Earth are also suspicious of ID positions that compromise on evolution and make God out to be involved in the macroevolutionary process.

"Kinds" as "Species"

Theistic evolutionists would argue that the more Intelligent Design leans toward special creationism, the more it has the same problem with *kinds* and *species* as Young Earth and Old Earth.

Here's something to ponder about species, theistic evolutionists would argue: Beetles make up the most diverse order of organisms on the planet, with over 350,000 species; one-fifth of all known species are beetles. A clergyman once asked famed geneticist J. S. B. Haldane, "What inferences could be drawn about the nature of God from a study of his works?" The self-proclaimed atheist Haldane chose to mock the Christian idea that God has a special care for human beings. He replied, "An inordinate fondness for beetles."[103]

Haldane's remark begs the question: Who's to say that God considers the number of beetles "inordinate"? Besides, the reality of tons of beetles is no argument against God having an entirely appropriate fondness for humans—and everything else he's created!

Where to Draw the Line

Just as Old Earth opens the door to questions about how to interpret the Bible if not literally, so does ID. This problem is not unanswerable, but it requires doing some hard work in the area of hermeneutics, or the study of how to closely interpret texts, especially books of the Bible. In short, a really simplistic answer won't do.

Replaying Galileo

Even though its chief proponents are Christians, ID is not about establishing sweeping doctrinal orthodoxy in the scientific community. Rather, ID sees itself as simply seeking to identify entry points for the arguments that God created the diversity of life.

Even so, like Young Earth and Old Earth, from the beginning ID has been tied to religious anti-evolutionist arguments, and that can be tied, by opponents, to a Galileo-type of problem (wedded to one particular scientific theory).

The Extra Hoops Argument: Discipleship Plus Anti-Evolutionism

Intelligent Design is not as insistent as many young earthers and old earthers that you must be anti-evolutionist to be a strong Christian. However, it seems that a lot of people in the ID movement are going to the mat on this issue. They've chosen this hill to die on because, as they see it, serious Christian commitment can barely go alongside belief in Darwinism.

Missing the Main Message of Genesis 1

Like Young Earth and Old Earth, ID's insistence on anti-evolutionism can be accused of distracting from the main message of Genesis 1, which, it can be argued, is less about the *what* and *how* of creation, and more about the *who* and *why*.

Relying on "Fringe Science"

The arguments for Intelligent Design carry a great deal of weight to people looking for a role for God in the evolutionary process. However, the logic of ID has not caught on with working biologists, many of whom are believers. Theistic evolutionist Francis Collins says, "Intelligent Design remains a fringe activity with little credibility within the mainstream scientific community."[104] Collins points out that scientific theories try to predict experimental observations. They look forward, not backward. ID fails to do this, he argues. Therefore, ID is "a scientific dead end," according to Collins.[105]

Lame Nay-Saying

Many in the ID movement try to falsify evolution. Unfortunately, their counterarguments against evolution are seen as repeats of the Old Earth and Young Earth charges.

Still No Fossil Rabbits in the Precambrian

None of the anti-evolutionist approaches have provided any "fossil rabbits in the Precambrian" or any other slam-dunk proofs against evolutionary order. So the form of ID that emphasizes special creation has the same problem as Young Earth and Old Earth: why would God "specially create" so much evidence of evolutionary trial-and-error leading to higher forms of life?

Massive Extinctions

The special creationist forms of ID can be said to face another hurdle also shared by Young Earth and Old Earth. The question, from the perspective of Theistic Evolution, is: If God specially designed and created each and every irreducibly complex biological system as well as each and every irreducibly complex species, what was the point of massive, worldwide extinctions?

> ID SEES ITSELF AS SIMPLY SEEKING TO IDENTIFY ENTRY POINTS FOR THE ARGUMENTS THAT **GOD CREATED THE DIVERSITY OF LIFE.**

Those holding to a Young Earth or Old Earth view argue that the Genesis flood account gives us clear reasoning why God allowed total destruction on the earth.

Sleeping Genes and Non-Irreducible Complexity

The amazing advances in genome studies may provide problems for the special-creation forms of ID. For example, ID does not explain how God's supernatural interventions might have produced complexity. Behe has proposed that simple organisms were "preloaded" with genetic information, but no such "sleeping genes" have been found.[106]

Collins puts forth what he sees as another problem for ID: "[I]t now seems likely that many examples of irreducible complexity are not irreducible after all, and that the primary scientific argument for ID is thus in the process of crumbling."[107] He then provides what he believes are direct counterexamples to ID's strongest arguments for irreducible complexity, including human blood-clotting, the eye, and even against one of the main arguments of ID, the bacterial flagellum.[108]

Evolution as Inherently Antispiritual

From the start, along with Young Earth and Old Earth, ID's driving assumption has been that evolution is based in philosophical naturalism/materialism/atheism; that evolution's idea of common descent removes spiritual dignity from humanity; and that, therefore, making peace with Darwinism naively caves in to naturalism.

However, Theistic Evolution would argue that these are not logically necessary conclusions because:

- *methodological naturalism in science is not the same as philosophical naturalism;*
- *common descent is biological, not spiritual;*
- *belief in evolution doesn't necessarily corrode faith;*
- *accepting evolution does not necessarily make one a surrender monkey.*

The "God of the Gaps" Problem

Intelligent Design's connection with the "God of the Gaps" argument was seen earlier in the "Sleeping Genes" section. ID can also be taken to task for possibly being wedded to a particular scientific theory.

Stealth Creationism

In the 1980s creation science lost some major court battles. Intelligent Design became an alternate strategy to bring God back into the public schools without violating the law. ID presented itself as nonreligious and

NATURAL THEOLOGY: A theology that holds that knowledge of God can be acquired by human reason, apart from the aid of divine revelation.

scientific, but its arguments against evolution, such as the "gaps" in the fossil record, were seen as older creation science strategies. Because ID proponents were reluctant to name the intelligent designer, critics began calling it stealth creationism.

Natural Theology as Misguided

Another objection to ID comes from a (perhaps) unexpected quarter: reformed Christian theology.

Some background: In Christian history, the argument for the existence of God from design has always been part of something bigger, labeled by some as natural theology. Many have sought to ground belief in God in what can be termed general revelation (and reason alone), which is different from special revelation.

Some definitions: General revelation is about the truth of God's power and existence being available to all people through nature itself. The Bible makes this argument forcefully in Romans 1:18-20. It also should be seen through the fact that we live in a moral universe, which the apostle Paul argues strongly in Romans 2. The first two chapters of Romans, in fact, tell us we are all accountable to God because of this dual witness.

Special revelation can be defined as supernatural insight given by God that reveals our desperate need for forgiveness, and how Jesus Christ has fulfilled that need. Special revelation takes more than human wisdom—it is an act of intervention on God's part.

The sixteenth-century Protestant Reformers Martin Luther and John Calvin rejected general revelation, teaching that human reason—because it is corrupted by sin—would inevitably misread or obscure the truth about God and what he was like. (For them, special revelation would be needed to find those truths.) To this day some inheritors of the Reformation steadfastly reject as misguided all forms of natural theology, including those held by the contemporary Intelligent Design movement.[109]

12 CHIMPS, AHOY!

And the king, looking at what I had written, read with astonishment and exclaimed,
Can an ape possess such fluency and such skill in calligraphy?
—THE ARABIAN NIGHTS (1909)

Your last visit to the zoo, when you went to the great ape exhibit, did you get up close and stare into the eyes of any of the apes? How did that make you feel? Did you wonder what was going on behind those eyes that looked so similar to yours, yet so different?

Jane Goodall, who spent decades studying the family and social life of

JANE GOODALL EXPERIENCED EYEBALL-TO-EYEBALL ENCOUNTERS LIKE THAT IN THE WILD. IN ONE EPISODE, SHE FOLLOWED A MEMBER OF THE CLAN INTO THE JUNGLE.

chimpanzees in Gombe National Park in what is now Tanzania, experienced eyeball-to-eyeball encounters like that in the wild. In one episode, she followed a member of the clan into the jungle. There by a stream, she says:

I found him sitting by the water, almost as if he were waiting for me. I looked into his large and lustrous eyes, set so wide apart; they seemed somehow to express his entire personality, his serene self-assurance, his inherent dignity. . . . His eyes seemed almost like windows through which, if only I had the skill, I could look into his mind.[110]

Goodall didn't just spend all her time staring into the eyes of chimpanzees. She also discovered chimpanzees stripping leaves off small branches, poking the modified branches into termite mounds, patiently waiting a bit, then carefully pulling the twigs out, now covered with termites. Into the chimp's mouths the twigs would go. Mmmmm, yummy good eatin'!

But also, this was rudimentary toolmaking! Goodall had witnessed, for the first time, animals other than humans making tools. Before this time, it had been widely thought that humans alone were toolmakers. Goodall sent the news to Louis Leakey, her mentor working with human-like fossils in Ethiopia. He famously responded, "Ah! We must now redefine man, redefine tool, or accept chimpanzees as human!"[111]

Leakey's comment, playful as it was, pointed to the revolutionary nature of Goodall's study. She wrote:

"My observations at Gombe challenged human uniqueness, and whenever that happens there is always a violent scientific and theological uproar." Some people accused her of training the chimps to fish for termites with twigs.

However, the photographic evidence she supplied eventually put that accusation to rest. But still the question remains: What distinguishes humans from chimps and the animal kingdom? As Goodall said, "Heaven forbid that we should lose any aspect of our human uniqueness!"[112]

This illustrates one important religious and philosophical question in the Late Great Ape Debate: What does it mean to be human? If we were related to apes by an apelike/humanlike earlier ancestor, would that take away from our being made in God's image?

Let's flesh out a typical Theistic Evolution interpretation of Genesis 1-3.

- *Genesis 1 would be taken as a story that would have communicated powerfully within the assumptions of how the universe came to be among people in the ancient Near East.*

- *Genesis 2 would be taken as a story to elaborate the teaching in Genesis 1 that we are created in God's image. When Genesis 2:7 says "God . . . breathed into (Adam's) nostrils the breath of life, and the man became a living being," instead of taking this to mean that God literally brought physical human life to a clay figure, Trinitarian theistic evolutionists take the verse to mean that at some early stage of human development, God breathed a spiritual awareness into beings on earth who had the physical characteristics of humans, but were not yet fully human. Admittedly from this viewpoint, this view is speculative, since no person could know for sure when or how this might have happened.*

- *In Genesis 3, the fall of man would not necessarily be taken as an historical, one-time event, but could be suggestive of all humans at all times and in all societies, telling about the universal problem of innocence lost and our willingness to put self over God and others.[113]*

- *In this view, sin is not seen as being transferred biologically, but socially and spiritually; we inherit social structures of injustice and patterns of selfish behavior.*

- *There is not an insistence that a worldwide flood must be taken as historical, but it can be viewed as allegory, perhaps as a distant memory of an ancient devastating flood sent as punishment from God. We have seen, with the Christmas tsunami in Asia (2004) and Hurricane Rita in New Orleans (2005), how floodwaters can completely erase whole communities.*

Tensions arise with each of the points above and certain biblical passages, but Trinitarian Theistic Evolution believes these tensions can be resolved in a fully orthodox way. (Unless otherwise noted, in this chapter TE will refer to Trinitarian Theistic Evolution, a Theistic Evolution that embraces one eternal God who has always existed as God the Father, God the Son, and God the Holy Spirit—the God of the Bible.)

Let's move on to the positives and difficulties for Theistic Evolution.

POSITIVES FOR THEISTIC EVOLUTION

Trinitarian Theistic Evolution maintains the basic biblical worldview of God as creator, Jesus as Savior, and God acting in his world. TE recognizes the importance of discerning the biblical worldview from the other worldviews.

Theistic evolutionists respect the clear, simple teachings of Scripture, and see their views as compatible with the Bible as authoritative Scripture. Yet they don't insist the Bible must be taken literally at every point, nor that its intent is to give us accurate scientific knowledge. Nor do proponents insist that modern science is the authoritative road to truth. Combining these thoughts, this plays out in a resistance to the temptation to seek to have the Bible inserted into science classes.[114] (Theistic Evolution regards history as recorded human history; essentially, what has been penned from eyewitness account, or handed down from eyewitnesses. This removes the creation story in Genesis and the second coming of Christ from "history," strictly speaking, because no human eyewitness was writing down a blow-by-blow account of the creation, and no human eye can see into the future. As such, TE would argue that the rules for interpreting those two colossal events at either pole of the Bible are different from other texts that come to us rooted in real-time human events.)

Theistic evolutionists will argue that they preserve a special place for humanity as created in the image of God.

TE respects Jesus' attitude toward the authority of the Old Testament as God's Word.

TE respects the grand narrative of Scripture—the creation, fall, and redemption of humans.

TE accepts that God is all-powerful and wise, and that God has a design and a purpose for creation. But TE also would choose to leave room for macroevolution in how God's design and purposes work out. Theistic evolutionists would argue that God is continuously creating through the process of evolution, even at this moment.

Like Young Earth, Old Earth, and Intelligent Design, TE upholds the Bible as our moral compass—anchored by the Ten Commandments (Exodus 20:1-17) and Jesus' teaching on the two greatest commandments (Matthew 22:37-39)—and calls for human accountability to God.

TE looks at nature as amazingly equipped by God with characteristics that inherently provide for immense diversity. The other Christian approaches would share this view, of course, but in a way that looks through a non-macroevolution lens.

> THEISTIC EVOLUTION ALSO INTRODUCES SOME **TOUGH** QUESTIONS, AMBIGUITIES, AND UNCERTAINTIES.

Theistic evolutionists are unthreatened by the methodological naturalism of science.

TE argues that if macroevolution is true, then not all things are predetermined. Mutations in DNA happen on a regular basis. In the sovereignty of God, there is room for randomness and indeterminacy.

TE will argue that evolution is the master theory upon which all the biological sciences are based, and that these sciences also agree with many other disciplines, such as geology, radiometric dating techniques, and astronomy.

But Theistic Evolution also introduces some tough questions, ambiguities, and uncertainties.

DIFFICULTIES FOR THEISTIC EVOLUTION

Now we turn to the difficulties that theistic evolutionists face as seen through the eyes of Young Earth Creationism, Old Earth Creationism, and Intelligent Design.

The Battery of Anti-Evolution Arguments

TE must face all the arguments that the other three Christian positions bring up against Naturalistic Evolution. A partial list is: God wouldn't lie; the plain and simple meaning of the Bible is apparent; *kinds* should be taken as *species*; the gaps in the fossil record; evolution's randomness cannot explain the diversity and complexity we see in the universe; loss of the image of God if humans and apes have a common ancestor; the Bible's account of Noah's flood (Genesis 6–9) explains the earth's great geologic formations, such as the Grand Canyon; the problems that Young Earth raises against an old earth; conflict with the second law of thermodynamics, or entropy (see the discussion in chapter 3); problems with various dating techniques; the concept of irreducible complexity in living beings; and the anthropic principle.

> **ANTHROPIC PRINCIPLE:** Two main principles are offered on how things came to exist: the *weak anthropic principle* says that observable conditions in the universe make it a given that the observer must exist; the *strong anthropic principle* says the universe's obvious properties make it inevitable that there must be an intelligent designer.

The Piltdown Meltdown

At one time, Piltdown man was seen as one of the twentieth century's biggest "discoveries," its finders alleging it to be "the missing link" between humans and apes. But as things turned out, Piltdown was a hoax and became the last century's biggest scientific humiliation.[115] Whenever arguments against human evolution come up, proponents of the other views often quickly bring the Piltdown fraud to the table.

A Slippery Slope

No matter how TE might be presented, many Christians view it as thinly disguised naturalism, as a front for secular humanism, atheism, and other similar worldviews.

People have lost their faith over the issue of human evolution vs. non-human evolution. Charles Darwin himself was one who moved from faith

THE FAMOUS PILTDOWN MAN HOAX: From 1911 to 1915, in Piltdown, a village in Sussex, England, amateur geologist Charles Dawson and his friend, Arthur Woodward, supposedly discovered a fossilized skull, partial jawbone, and two teeth of a hominid ancestor that were hailed as proof that the missing link between apes and humans had been found.

The only problem was, Piltdown was an elaborate forgery. It was so clever, and so matched the expectations of scientists, that it fooled much of the scientific community for nearly forty years.

In 1953, scientists from Oxford University and the British Museum conclusively proved that Piltdown man was a fraud. The skull fragment had been stolen from a museum, the identifying marks broken or filed off. The jaw fragment also had been stolen; it was of a recently deceased female orangutan. The fragments had been stained brown to make them look old.

As a result, science got a black eye—and hundreds of thousands of school textbooks had to be changed.

in God as designer to a belief in survival of the fittest, natural selection, and random mutations. He switched from the biblical worldview to the worldview of naturalism.

Other former Christians who have bought into evolution have moved into process theology,[116] which says that God, like his creation, is in process; he is evolving. The god of process theology is part of his creation; he doesn't have unilateral authority over it. This god may be good and loving, but he's not all-powerful. In other words, he's just doing the best he can.

PROCESS THEOLOGY: The belief that God, like his creation, is evolving. It holds that God does not exert unilateral control over the universe; his powers are limited merely to passive persuasion.

Process theology is a watered-down version of pantheism, the worldview belief that everything is "one" or everything is spirit. In pantheism everything (including God) eventually boils down to an Impersonal Absolute. Not content with an absolutely impersonal god, process theology tries to infuse its god with a veneer of personality. A pathetic attempt, this is a far, far cry from the Christian understanding of one all-powerful and good God, forever having existed as God the Father, God the Son, and God the Holy Spirit.

Trashing the Uniqueness of Biblical Revelation

As we've seen, some theistic evolutionists are not Trinitarians; some theistic evolutionists do not have a high regard for the Jewish and Christian Scriptures. They treat the Bible merely as an ancient book full of long-since-out-of-date fables.

Very common among such people is belief in a shapeless, generic, unnamed, and unnamable God: some might call him Allah, or the Great Spirit, or any of a thousand names—it doesn't matter.

The feeling among a lot of Christians in the Young Earth, Old Earth, and Intelligent Design camps is that little in Theistic Evolution prevents people from moving in this direction.

> MANY CHRISTIANS SIMPLY CANNOT IMAGINE A SCENARIO IN WHICH "FROM GOO TO YOU" COULD RESULT IN **HUMANS BEING CREATED IN THE IMAGE OF GOD WITH INNATE DIGNITY AND WORTH.**

Compromising Biblical Authority

The other approaches look at TE as compromising on biblical authority. If theistic evolutionists choose to take Genesis 1 as an allegory, or poetry, or even a myth—or something else—a cascade of other important questions tumble down. What about other parts of the Bible? If TE holds that Genesis 1 is not literal history, then what about the Exodus, David and Solomon, and the resurrection of Christ? Was Jesus himself fallible or a legend? On what basis, looking from the perspectives of the texts themselves, can historical truth be separated from something written that is only based on truth or from something written that is entirely fiction?

Mocking Intelligent Design: A Dangerous Path to Take

Naturalistic evolutionists who reject God often scoff at the whole idea of an intelligent designer. They call inactive DNA junk DNA. They call the design of the human spine incompetent because so many people develop lower back pain. Or they bring up the appendix, which has a significant function in rabbits but has long been seen as having no function in humans (although research in recent years is pointing to several possible benefits of the organ, including an immunological one in adults[xiv]). They say that God must have been asleep at the switch when he made us. Unfortunately, some proponents of Theistic Evolution who are Christians find it all too easy to use the same kinds of naturalistic arguments to bash the faith, integrity, and intelligence of other Christians who doubt Darwinism.

Common Descent as Repellant

Many Christians simply cannot imagine a scenario in which "from goo to you" could result in humans being created in the image of God with innate dignity and worth. The visceral reaction against the idea of apes and humans having a common ancestor and all of life going back to earlier life forms seems to them a ghastly, ungodly thought that contradicts Scripture. They might point to Mark 10:6, for instance.

Also, at the very heart of Christian teaching is the belief that we are not just accidents of time, chance, and matter. We are created by God and loved. TE's idea of randomness (at many levels) and the Bible telling us that God cares for each of us individually seem to be in conflict.

Loss of the Grand Biblical Narrative

The other approaches look suspiciously at what they see as Theistic Evolution's reinterpretation of the grand biblical narrative of original perfect creation, the fall of man and spread of spiritual and physical death, and redemption

---

[xiv] See the ABC News article "Scientists discover true function of appendix organ" at www.abc.net.au/news/stories/2007/10/10/2055374.htm.

through Christ. Proponents of the other views would say that, if human evolution is true, a perfect creation is a myth, and the fall didn't really happen in history. So, they ask, what's to keep TE from radically and nonhistorically reinterpreting the resurrection of Jesus as well?

The Original Brutality of Nature

Nature is beautiful and awesome, to be sure. But it can also be brutal. Every living thing depends for its life on the death of other living things. Think of clips like those on TV's *Wild Kingdom* of a great white shark munching down on a dozing seal by the seashore, or the wild-eyed and helpless look of the wildebeest as it's taken down as dinner by the charging lion.

So the problem is: how do you reconcile a good God with all the animal suffering needed to bring about evolution—a new wrinkle on the old problem of how God could allow such pain and suffering in the world for humans.

The Plain, Simple Meaning of the Text

To those who hold to a traditional Christian understanding of the grand narrative of perfect creation, fall of man, and redemption, any attempts to reinterpret things to make allowance for the possibility of death before the fall seem to be special pleading and doomed because they don't hold to the plain, simple meaning of the Bible.

A Hands-Off God

People who believe in macroevolution and also believe in God would seem to have a view of God in which he is very hands-off. The other Christian views choose to think of God as far more hands-on and vitally interested in creation and what's going on here in the physical realm.

In this regard, many Christians are suspicious that the God of theistic evolutionists is a god of deism, aloof and unconcerned for his creation and the people in it. If God isn't near to us and concerned for us as the Bible clearly teaches, why pray and expect him to answer?

A Loss of God's Sovereignty

The Bible has a lot to say about God's sovereignty and rulership over the affairs of men. (Read the book of Daniel if you ever doubt the Bible's claims about this!) Arguments can be made that if common descent is true and mutations happen randomly, God can no longer be considered sovereign. This would seem to contradict Scripture (compare Psalm 139:13-16; 148:5), which says that chaos and disorder do not rule—God does.

Putting Human Reason over Faith

Many Christians believe that to accept macroevolution you have to put human agendas and human reason over God's revelation in Scripture. They would regard doing such a thing an affront to true reason, which calls for putting God and his truth first. Since God wouldn't lie, it only makes sense to trust God, rather than our own understanding (Proverbs 3:5, 6).

THE FEELING AMONG MANY ANTI-EVOLUTIONIST CHRISTIANS IS THAT **EVOLUTION IS SHEER PROPAGANDA** SOLD BY PROPONENTS OF THE NATURALISTIC WORLDVIEW.

Succumbs to Propaganda

The feeling among many anti-evolutionist Christians is that evolution is sheer propaganda sold by proponents of the naturalistic worldview. Those scientists who are pro-Theistic Evolution are either duped or propagandists, the other Christian views would say.

What About the Youth?

Surely, a key issue at play here is the spiritual message relayed to youth. The thinking on the part of many Christians is that Darwin's theory of evolution is just too based in materialistic philosophy and just too dangerous to favor acceptance on any level. The fear is that saying yes to evolution—whether Trinitarian TE or any form of Darwinism taught in a public school science class—will cause all kinds of spiritual havoc down the line.

Undercuts the Basis for Morality

Darwinism has caused many people to lose a sense of God's presence, to question biblical standards of morality, and to act in ways that seem "right in [their] own eyes" (Judges 17:6, *NKJV*) and exclude God. Evolution has been used to pry the culture apart from Christian morality. It has been used to bash religion (especially Christianity), to promote free sex (which has led to immense health and social problems), to attempt to turn society into an economic jungle, and to justify racial superiority, slavery, even genocide. It's ended in places like marriage no longer being viewed as sacred, or people hooking up any time they feel the urge. Stepping over or on others is OK because natural selection tells us it's all about survival of the fittest. Sociobiology tells us we're just doing what our selfish genes are telling us to do. These attitudes are obviously inconsistent with Christianity's high standards of morality and the universal moral teachings of many religions in general.

"The Devil's Strategy"

For many Christians, TE is fraught with peril; they bring out the heavy artillery to gun it down. From www.gospelway.com (a "Bible online religion guide"): "Any compromise with evolution leads inevitably to a rejection of Bible teaching."[117] And from the Christian resource Web site www.livingtheway.org: "Evolution is the Devil's most powerful modern weapon."[118]

For some believers, the battle lines are drawn. There is no way to have the Bible and Darwinism.

DANCESWITHAPES

13 INHERITTHESPIN

Let's go back to the famous Scopes "Monkey" Trial in Dayton, Tennessee, in the blistering hot month of July 1925. By the twist of fate that we talked about in chapter 1, the prosecuting attorney, William Jennings Bryan, is actually on the witness stand, being questioned by the defense attorney, Clarence Darrow.

Or is that exactly the case? In the dialogue below, from a fictionalized account of that piece of history, Matthew Harrison Brady is actually Bryan's character, and Henry Drummond is Darrow.

Hang on tightly, because you are about to enter the world of major-league spin:

Matthew Harrison Brady: We must not abandon faith! Faith is the most important thing!

Henry Drummond: Then why did God plague us with the capacity to think? Mr. Brady, why do you deny the one thing that sets [man] above the other animals? What other merit have we? The elephant is larger, the horse stronger and swifter, the butterfly more beautiful, the mosquito more prolific, even the sponge is more durable. Or does a sponge think?

Brady: I don't know. I'm a man, not a sponge!

Drummond: Do you think a sponge thinks?

Brady: If the Lord wishes a sponge to think, it thinks!

Drummond: Does a man have the same privilege as a sponge?

Brady: Of course!

Drummond [gesturing toward the defendant, Bertram Cates]: Then this man wishes to have the same privilege of a sponge, he wishes to think!

—FROM THE MOVIE *INHERIT THE WIND* (1960)

Today, we associate spin with presidential candidates and other politicians, with wars, with our fallen sports heroes. But spin has been around for a long time. Spin, in the form of Jerome Lawrence and Robert E. Lee's fictional play, is all the "memory" most people have of *The State of Tennessee v. John Thomas Scopes*. The play hit Broadway in 1955, was made into a major motion picture in 1960, and has undergone three reincarnations as TV movies (1965, 1988, 1999).

Inherit the Wind has not been without controversy. Some have called it propaganda, an unfair manipulation of history. Others have called it a great American play. Several generations of students have watched it and written papers about it. If you haven't seen the original movie, I recommend it highly. Whatever else one thinks of it, it is a piece of Americana.

But what is it: propaganda or art? If propaganda, shouldn't we examine the motives of the playwrights and call them to account for spreading misleading falsehoods? And if art, shouldn't we give those same playwrights a pass? After all, to heighten the drama, don't plays and movies always stretch the truth some? Why not call it artistic license and let it go?

Fair questions! To try to form an answer, let's compare the play with the historical record.[119]

THE PLAY	THE HISTORICAL RECORD
The Setting and Characters Setting: Hillsboro, Tennessee Science teacher: Bertram Cates	 Setting: Dayton, Tennessee Science teacher: John Scopes

THE PLAY	THE HISTORICAL RECORD
Defense attorney: Henry Drummond	Defense attorney: Clarence Darrow
The reporter: E. K. Hornbeck of the *Baltimore Herald*; the Herald paid him to cover the trial.	The reporter: H. L. Mencken of the *Baltimore Evening Sun*; the Sun helped pay for Scopes's defense.
The prosecuting attorney: Matthew Harrison Brady, a great orator, populist leader, three-time presidential candidate—and leader of the crusade against evolution	The prosecuting attorney: William Jennings Bryan, a great orator, thirty-year leader in the Democratic party, and three-time candidate for president as a populist—but he was not a leader of the crusade against evolution
THE MAIN STORY Cates is a knowledgeable science teacher.	Scopes coached football and taught math. Scopes never taught evolution; for two weeks he was a substitute biology teacher. His students knew more about evolution than he did. The defense kept him off the stand to avoid embarrassment.
Cates has already been arrested and is in jail. (In the 1960 film's opening sequence, Cates is arrested by a grim posse of morally offended citizens.)	Scopes never went to jail. He was free to travel. He went to New York to meet with American Civil Liberties Union executives. He continued to live in Dayton and was on a friendly basis with many people in the town.
Cates was brought up on charges that he had taught evolution, which was against the law.	Tennessee's Butler Act made it illegal to teach the descent of man from apes and forbade public school teachers to deny the Bible's account of creation. However, no effort was ever made to enforce the Butler Act, and the Butler Act did not call for a prison penalty.

THE PLAY	THE HISTORICAL RECORD
	. . . What actually happened—and went unmentioned in the play—was that the ACLU wanted to challenge the Butler Act in court and advertised to find someone to be its legal guinea pig. The ACLU persuaded Scopes to be their guy by paying his way for a degree in geology from the University of Chicago.
	William Jennings Bryan's kindness and sincerity were acknowledged even by his enemies. Bryan spoke in a friendly way with Scopes, insisting they could be friends despite their legal disagreement.
Henry Drummond derides the honorific title of Colonel that the town bestows on his rival, Brady.	Fiction. "Colonel" was a customary honorary title in the courtroom and was extended to all legal counsel in the Scopes case, including Darrow.
	Also, Bryan had earned the position of colonel in the US Army during the Spanish-American War (although he never saw combat).
The newspaperman Hornbeck heaps abuse on what he sees as ignorance and bigotry. He belittles Brady's fundamentalism.	One of the rare cases where art matched real life: The newspaperman Mencken belittled Bryan, calling him "a tinpot pope in the coca-cola belt." The typical newspaper stories coming out of the trial enjoyed making Bryan look bad.
The townspeople shun Drummond and a little girl screams "Devil!" at him. The film portrays a scowling hillbilly. Courtroom spectators clearly side with Brady.	. . . What actually happened: Darrow was greeted by a crowd almost as large and friendly as the one that greeted Bryan. Both were invited to the Progressive Club dinner. Darrow won over many of the locals, and many courtroom spectators sided with the defense.

THE PLAY	THE HISTORICAL RECORD
In the film, the people of Hillsboro are portrayed as ignorant, lacking courtesy, and threatening to Cates, the defense lawyers, and any outsiders.	. . . What actually happened: Darrow wrote, "I don't know as I was ever in a community in my life where my religious ideas differed as widely from the great mass as I have found them since I have been in Tennessee. Yet I came here a perfect stranger and I can say . . . that I have not found upon anybody's part—any citizen here in this town or outside . . . the slightest discourtesy. I have been treated better, kindlier and more hospitably than I fancied would have been the case in the north."
Cates is a sturdy individualist fighting a lonely battle against small-town bigotry.	. . . What actually happened: Besides Darrow, Scopes was represented by Arthur Garfield Hays of the ACLU, divorce lawyer Dudley Field Malone, and constitutional expert John Randolph Neal. Scopes wrote later that he couldn't have done better if he'd had all the money in the world.
Cates experiences fear and trembling in his prison cell, the threat of isolation and complete ruin hanging over his head. He loses his job.	. . . What actually happened: Scopes's job was still open to him after the trial. But the defense had offered him a scholarship to study geology at the University of Chicago, which Scopes accepted. (He went on to have an active career as a geologist.) During one lunch recess in the trial, Scopes went swimming with two of the young assistant prosecutors, one of whom was Bryan's son. For that stunt, the biggest reprimand for Scopes in the entire trial likely came from his own attorneys.
An announcement is made for an evening prayer meeting at the end of the first day of the trial.	Fiction. However, Darrow objected to the use of prayer at the opening of every trial day, as was the custom in Tennessee (and is the custom to this day in the United States Supreme Court).

THE PLAY	THE HISTORICAL RECORD
Defense attorney Drummond introduces Darwin's Descent of Man into evidence as an evolution textbook used by Scopes.	Clear fiction. . . . What actually happened: It was the prosecuting attorney Bryan who introduced the evolution textbook (Hunter's *Civic Biology*) into evidence.
Drummond, desperate to challenge the law with which Cates is accused, flatters Brady into taking the stand as an expert on the Bible. This testimony turns the case around.	Bryan did take the stand, but he was not flattered into it. It was a mistake, but he felt he needed to take Darrow up on his challenge or find himself acknowledging that his position could not be defended. In the witness box he said, "These gentlemen came here to try revealed religion. I am here to defend it, and they can ask me any questions they please."
Drummond accuses Brady of believing that original sin is sexual intercourse.	Fiction. Sex never came up.
Drummond closely questions Brady on the date of creation being 4004 BC.	Fiction. Bryan never quoted Bishop Ussher's date.
Drummond is presented as a reasonable and fair-minded person.	Darrow was clearly a man with an agenda. He described his role as "preventing bigots and ignoramuses from controlling the education of the United States."
Drummond exposes Brady's literal acceptance of the Bible as indefensible. Drummond has to work hard to get Brady to say he doesn't believe in the literal "days" of the Genesis creation account.	Bryan was not a young earth creationist. He volunteered his view that the "days" of Genesis were not 24-hour days. He did not insist that the sun literally stood still (see Joshua 10:13), but explained that the Bible was using the language of the time. Despite aggressive and intense questioning, Bryan did not waver in his belief in miracles and the supremacy of God's power.

THE PLAY	THE HISTORICAL RECORD
Drummond makes a big deal about Brady's status as a self-appointed prophet.	More fiction. Bryan never made such a claim.
The courtroom is packed during Brady's testimony.	. . . What actually happened: The courtroom was sparsely attended. Only six reporters bothered to attend Darrow's famous cross-examination.
Brady is portrayed as flummoxed and overmatched.	Trial transcripts reveal that Bryan was often exuberant, funny, discerning, and focused. He was familiar with Darwin's theories and knew what was at stake. He had some embarrassing moments during Darrow's questioning, but he often gave as good as he got.
Brady is crushed by the experience.	Fiction. Bryan was never personally crushed. However, anti-evolutionism suffered a major embarrassment.
Brady seeks comfort from his wife. Later that evening, she cradles him and coos "Baby, baby." The jury brings home a guilty verdict.	Bryan's wife was a semi-invalid. He was very protective of her. . . . What actually happened: Defense attorney Darrow entered a guilty plea for Scopes so the case could go more quickly to appeals. A year later, the guilty verdict was overturned on a technicality. (Nearly a half-century later, in 1968, several other states' laws similar to the Butler Act were declared unconstitutional.)
The judge fines Cates $100.	Another rare case where art matched life: The judge fined Scopes $100. However . . . Bryan argued against the fine and even offered to pay it for Scopes.

THE PLAY	THE HISTORICAL RECORD
Brady tries to protest, but loses all dignity in a lengthy and incoherent tirade. The judge ends the trial.	. . . What actually happened: Bryan never gave his closing statement, and it was not because of the judge. Rather, after Darrow's cross-examination of Bryan, the defense attorney moved to enter the guilty plea. Darrow later admitted that the defense wanted to deprive Bryan of his statement because of his legendary powers of speech.
Brady collapses then and there, and dies a short time later.	. . . What actually happened: Bryan did not collapse in the courtroom. But five days after the guilty verdict, he did die. The stress of the trial may have had something to do with it, but he also had a diabetic condition that he did not always carefully watch.
Hornbeck says, "He died of a busted belly," a cynical and cruel comment based on Brady's physical appearance.	. . . What actually happened: The de-rogatory comment from the play was actually spoken by Darrow when he learned that Bryan had died.
THE SUBPLOT	
Cates has a love interest. Rachel, his fiancée, is the daughter of a fire-and-brimstone preacher named Jeremiah Brown. Reverend Brown prays vengeful prayers just before the trial.	Complete fiction. The love-and-family story was entirely made up.
The fictional Rachel must choose between her family and small-town values, and love.	See above.

THE PLAY	THE HISTORICAL RECORD
Brady loses control and becomes mean and malicious in questioning Rachel on the stand. He tricks her into testifying that Cates is a non-believer. She realizes her mistake and decides to stand by Cates.	See above. In truth, no women participated in any aspect of the trial. It was actually Darrow who was condescending—even showed contempt for—witnesses, jurists, opposing attorneys, and the judge for what he perceived as their ignorance and narrow-mindedness. Darrow was cited for contempt of court.
BACK TO THE MAIN STORY	
The film version has the townspeople on a virtual witch hunt, burning Cates and Drummond in effigy and throwing rocks into Cates's cell. The play lacks these elements but still shows the people to be ugly and hateful.	Complete fiction.
After the trial, Drummond rebukes Hornbeck for his ridicule of Brady and fundamentalism.	Again, fiction. Darrow heaped abuse on Bryan before, during, and after the trial.
Drummond weighs Darwin's *On the Origin of Species* and the Bible and exits confidently with both books in his briefcase, as though he thinks both are equally valid.	Fiction. Darrow's contempt of the Bible and fundamentalism and his complete acceptance of evolution were apparent to everyone.

MONKEY TROUBLE

Inherit the Wind is a modern morality play. The playwrights Lawrence and Lee clearly had an objective. They wanted people to throw off religious authority, teaching, and biblical literalism, all of which they and others have equated with bigotry.

But to achieve their teaching objective, they had to play fast and furious with the facts.

For one thing, they completely left the American Civil Liberties Union out of the work, even though the ACLU was the major instigator of the case. Discerning readers will wonder: What agenda is behind the desire to conceal the ACLU's role? Was it just artistic? True, all plays have to cut their material to the bone. Or was calling attention to the ACLU's role something they wanted to avoid because it could weaken the tolerance angle? You must be the judge.

Then they had to give the hero role to the "good guys" (those for Darwinism) and the villain role to the "bad guys" (the fundamentalists). So they made the Drummond character, representing Clarence Darrow, into a fair-minded, rational, and likable fellow—the guy who in

> TO ACHIEVE THEIR TEACHING OBJECTIVE, THEY HAD TO **PLAY FAST AND FURIOUS WITH THE FACTS.**

real life railed at, ranted against, and roughly attacked all fundamentalists. They made the character representing William Jennings Bryan (Brady in the play) into an unsympathetic, bigoted, odious personality—the same person who in real life was accomplished, respected, and known everywhere for his graciousness, thoughtfulness, and kindness. They decided to keep the more complex Bryan out of the picture. In reality, Bryan was a political progressive who gained his energy by a strong spirit of evangelical fervor and power-to-the-people populism.

The stage directions for the play also serve to ridicule Bryan's character and the people who believe, like him, in the Bible: "It is important to the concept of the play that the town is visible always, looming there, as much on trial as the individual defendant."[xv]

The play puts the Scopes character—representing the independently minded thinker—in jail, while the unthinking "morons" of the town roam free.

The play presents human evolution as a self-evident, undeniable truth. At one point Drummond says, "What Bertram Cates spoke quietly one spring afternoon in the Hillsboro High School is . . . [as] incontrovertible as geometry in every enlightened community of minds."

[xv] All quotes about the play following in this chapter are from Carol Iannone's "The Truth about *Inherit the Wind* (a play by Jerome Lawrence and Robert E. Lee)," in *First Things* (February 1997).

This sentiment echoes the real-life statement of ACLU lawyer Hays, who wrote that the trial "was a battle between two types of mind—the unyielding, narrow, conventional mind, and the broad, liberal, critical, cynical, skeptical, and tolerant mind." It also expresses the opinion of the one scientific expert to testify, Maynard M. Metcalf, a Johns Hopkins University professor (and theistic evolutionist), who said (from the transcript of the trial itself) that it would be impossible for "a normal human being, cognizant of the facts, to have the slightest doubt" about the fact of human evolution. These kinds of take-no-prisoners statements, magnified by the press, built on each other to create the stereotype that only those who are against evolution are intolerant and narrow-minded. But the problem cuts both ways.

To illustrate the double-talk that often masquerades as tolerance, the following words come from Drummond, the Darrow character, at the death of the Bryan character: "A giant once lived in that body. But Matt Brady got lost. Because he was looking for God too high up and too far away." Kind of preachy, but a decent enough thought given to the Darrow character by Lawrence and Lee. After Bryan's death, Darrow actually said that his opponent was "the moron of all Morondom."

> THE PLAYWRIGHTS MADE THE BRYAN CHARACTER INTO A BUMBLING LAUGHINGSTOCK. IN REALITY, **BRYAN WAS WORLDVIEW-SAVVY.**

In the play, the pious words Drummond had for Brady were not very consistent with his final speech in which he says, for the hilltop view that Darwin sought to teach, "We must abandon our faith in the pleasant poetry of Genesis." But in fact, Darrow was an unfaltering agnostic and only tried to show how Darwin had snuffed out the Bible.

When the Darrow character brought students from the high school to the witness stand, he asked, "Did [learning about evolution] hurt you any? Do you still believe in church although you were told all life comes from a single cell? . . . Haven't murdered anybody since breakfast?" With this line of questioning, the playwrights implied that there is no connection between philosophy and morals.

The playwrights made the Bryan character into a bumbling laughingstock. In reality, Bryan was worldview-savvy. A member of the American Academy for the Advancement of Science, he had misgivings about the materialist philosophy that many connected to evolution. He said, "The evolutionists have not been honest with the public. . . . Christians who have allowed themselves into believing that evolution is a beneficent, or even a rational, process have been associating with those who either do not understand its implications or dare not avow their knowledge of those implications." In saying this Bryan put his finger on a key problem for theistic evolutionists: If you accept evolutionary theory, is there room left for God? This is exactly the kind of perceptive worldview question that Christians need to be bringing to the table.

> HE SAID, "THE EVOLUTIONISTS HAVE NOT BEEN HONEST WITH THE PUBLIC." IN SAYING THIS BRYAN PUT HIS FINGER ON A KEY PROBLEM FOR THEISTIC EVOLUTIONISTS: IF YOU ACCEPT EVOLUTIONARY THEORY, IS THERE ROOM LEFT FOR GOD?

The last scene, in which Drummond puts both *On the Origin of Species* and the Bible into his briefcase and walks thoughtfully out of the room, seems to indicate that Lawrence and Lee, the play's authors, thought both godless cynicism and biblical fundamentalism were wrong, or at least equal. And with that last briefcase scene, the playwrights made Mencken, the newspaperman, into a cool, calm, and collected character. But as we know from his trial coverage, the real Mencken was a bigot who openly spewed hate and abuse on anyone who could possibly believe in the Bible.

THE REAL CHOICE: NOT AS EASY AS PEELING A BANANA

After comparing the play's portrayal of the Scopes Trial with the historical record, Carol Iannone wrote in her 1997 article "The Truth About *Inherit the Wind*":

> "Such a simple choice between bigotry and enlightenment is central to the contemporary liberal vision. . . . While it stands nominally for tolerance, latitude and freedom of thought, the play is full of the self-righteous certainty that it deplores in the fundamentalist camp."

Tolerance, latitude, freedom of thought: good in theory, but not always easy to achieve in personal practice, no matter who one is.

Is the choice really between "bigotry," in the form of traditional Christian belief (*if* we accept what Lawrence and Lee are selling), and "enlightenment," or naturalism (again, as seems to be the play's message)? And are Darwinism and Christian faith compatible, as the play's ending briefcase scene could be viewed as portraying?

Many Christians and many non-Christians, many anti-evolutionists and many pro-evolutionists would say no; they would say the two are irreconcilable.

Others would say that it depends on how you define Darwinism and how you define Christian faith.

So what do you say?

14 NOCHIMPLEFTBEHIND

It is the sense of the Senate that (1) good science education should prepare students to distinguish the data or testable theories of science from philosophical or religious claims that are made in the name of science; and (2) where biological evolution is taught, the curriculum should help students to understand why the subject generates so much continuing controversy, and should prepare the students to be informed participants in public discussions regarding the subject.
—THE PROPOSED (BUT NEVER ENACTED) SANTORUM AMENDMENT FOR THE NO CHILD LEFT BEHIND ACT (2001)

This is George.
He lived with his friend, the man with the yellow hat.
He was a good little monkey, but he was always curious.
—*CURIOUS GEORGE GOES TO THE HOSPITAL* (1966)

The amendment proposed by former U.S. senator Rick Santorum (Pennsylvania) to the famous education bill of 2001 became quite the lightning rod for controversy. It was driven by the Intelligent Design movement and has been summed up with the statement that its main goal was simply to state that there are disagreements in many scientific theories and that those theories are continually being tested.

I'm curious. Why all the fuss? The amendment looks reasonable.

And while we're at it, what's the status of attempts by Christians to make some room for God in public school science classrooms? How are things going on that front?

To answer these questions, we'll need to review the creation/evolution controversy through the lens of case law in the United States since the Scopes Trial. But before we do that, let's take a close look at an important law that underlies every legal battle since the debate began.

THE ESTABLISHMENT CLAUSE OF THE U.S. CONSTITUTION

According to the First Amendment to the Constitution of the United States (ratified in 1791):

> *Congress shall make no law respecting an establishment of religion, or prohibiting the free exercise thereof; or abridging the freedom of speech, or of the press; or the right of the people peaceably to assemble, and to petition the Government for a redress of grievances.*[120]

The Establishment Clause of the First Amendment (sometimes called the non-establishment clause) is that first phrase "shall make no law respecting an establishment of religion, or prohibiting the free exercise thereof." This amazing law decisively broke with 1,450 years of Western history, a pattern of theocratic politics that went all the way back to the fourth century, when the Roman emperor Constantine converted to Christianity and took the entire empire with him.

The American experiment wanted to get away from religious persecution and wars brought on by state religions. We fought a Revolution to make sure Britain didn't push the established church of England on us as the official

THEOCRACY: A government that approves, supports, favors, and enforces a particular religion and its laws; breaking religious laws, then, is viewed as treason.

religion. (Oh yes, taxes might have had something to do with it.) The Founding Fathers believed that the cornerstone of freedom is freedom of religion and, with it, freedom of conscience, which explains why the Establishment Clause is Item Number One in our national Bill of Rights.

We should notice that the Establishment Clause doesn't say, "Congress shall make no law *about* religion." The founders realized that some legal conflicts would inevitably touch on religious issues. Neither does the clause say, "Congress shall be biased toward secularism and be anti-religious," which would go directly against "or prohibiting the free exercise thereof." Rather, the founders wrote the clause to state, "Congress shall make no law *respecting an establishment of* religion." This makes all the difference. They didn't want the state playing favorites with any of the religious groups, and they absolutely wanted to make sure that Congress would never try to foist a state church on the American people. But the idea was also that the government would not involve itself in the area of religious expression.

As we think through the creation/evolution controversy in public schools, we need to remember that the relationship of church and state is intimately connected to the issue. Interestingly, there are some who think this whole discussion of church/state separation is absurd. They might argue that the Founding Fathers intended to set up a Christian religious state, with freedom of religion only for Christian denominations. They might argue that trying to have

SEPARATION OF CHURCH AND STATE: The political and legal idea that government and religious institutions should be separate and not interfere in each other's affairs. The term was coined by Thomas Jefferson (who certainly held this belief) in an 1802 letter to a Baptist group.

> JESUS DIDN'T MODEL A POLITICAL RELIGION—IN FACT, HE EXPRESSLY SAID THAT IS WHAT HE DID NOT COME TO SET UP (SEE JOHN 18:36).

a secular state promoting freedom of religion is an inherent contradiction. They might say we need to get back to an Old Testament-style theocracy. I'm not entirely sure of the basis for these types of thinking, but they're among the schools of thought.

Yes, as Christians we should mix it up in the marketplace of ideas and seek to persuade others from the Scriptures. Yes, we have every bit as much right as anyone else to take our most deeply held values to the public square. On the other hand, we're setting ourselves up for real conflict and disappointment if we think we can turn back the clock a few hundred years and make Christianity into something like an official state religion.

It should be said that many Christians are entirely comfortable with a clear separation of church and state. Jesus didn't model a political religion—in fact, he expressly said that is what he did *not* come to set up (see John 18:36). Christianity didn't start out as a state religion, and we shouldn't feel that we need church/state unity to do what Jesus wants us to do.

Now let's consider some of the major cases since 1925 that have played out at the center of the creation/evolution and church/state controversies.[121]

The Butler Act, Part I (1925–1967; Tennessee)

As we have seen, the Butler Act is the event that led to the Scopes Trial. It prohibited any public school teacher in Tennessee "to teach any theory that denies the story of the Divine Creation of man as taught in the Bible, and to teach instead that man has descended from a lower order of animals."[122] The ACLU challenged Butler and that was the end of that. Well, not exactly.

In fact, Butler had not been overturned. It stayed on the books, virtually unchallenged, for another forty-two years. In 1967 Gary L. Scott, a fresh-out-of-college science teacher, challenged Butler as an infringement to his free speech. Finally, the Tennessee legislature repealed the law. (See "The Butler Act, Part II, 1973–1975," below.)

Epperson v. Arkansas (1968)

This ruling by the United States Supreme Court struck down an Arkansas law that prohibited the teaching of evolution in public schools, effectively making all "monkey laws" unconstitutional. The Court said that the Arkansas law violated the Establishment Clause because it required teaching that is "tailored to the principles" of a particular religion.[123]

Lemon v. Kurtzman (1971; Pennsylvania)

This law allowed Pennsylvania to reimburse private and church schools for textbooks and teachers' salaries. The United States Supreme Court ruled that the practice violated the Establishment Clause and lacked a secular purpose. Out of this case the three-part "Lemon test" emerged:

- *The purpose of the aid could only be secular, not religious.*
- *The result could not aid, nor could it harm, religion.*
- *The result could not lead to excessive entanglement—basically, lots of oversight and rules—between the state and religion.*[124]

In short, the nation's high court was seeking to make clear the separation of church and state.

Wright v. Houston I.S.D. (1972; Texas)

Students in the Houston Independent School District sued the state for promoting evolution and violating their Establishment rights. The United States District Court of Texas, Southern Division, found the students' case unconvincing.[125]

> IN FACT, **BUTLER HAD NOT BEEN OVERTURNED.** IT STAYED ON THE BOOKS, VIRTUALLY UNCHALLENGED, FOR ANOTHER FORTY-TWO YEARS.

Willoughby v. Stever (1973; Washington, D.C. and Virginia)

William Willoughby, creationist, sued H. Guyford Stever, the National Science Foundation director, for improperly taking taxpayers' money to pay for evolution textbooks and for advocating secular humanism as the "official religion of the United States." The Washington, D.C. Circuit Court of Appeals dismissed the suit as not violating the Establishment Clause because the textbooks taught science, rather than a religion of secular humanism, according to the court.[126]

The Butler Act, Part II (1973–1975; Tennessee)

In 1973 the Tennessee legislature resurrected a form of the Butler Act in the so-called Genesis Bill (some called it Butler II), which said that no theory of creation or evolution could be presented as fact; all had to be presented as "theory," and each theory had to be given "equal time." Opposition immediately arose to the bill. The opponents claimed it put science and religion on equal footing, elevated a religious viewpoint to "science," and thus violated the Establishment Clause. Two years later in *Daniel v. Waters*, the U.S. Sixth District Court of Appeals struck down the bill.[127]

Segraves v. State of California (1981)

Three Segraves children and their father contended that discussion of evolution in the classroom violated the free exercise of religion for the children. The Sacramento Superior Court ruled that the California Board of Education's "Science Framework" had a policy against total acceptance of any one view that allowed discussing various statements (like creationism) about origins.[128] In short, the court ruled that the Segraves children's free exercise of religion had not been violated since various ideas on origins could be discussed in the classroom.

> THE RESULT IN ARKANSAS QUELLED THE **"EQUAL TIME MOVEMENT"** IN OTHER STATES.

McLean v. Arkansas Board of Education (1982)

From 1970–73, Russell Artist, a Bible teacher at David Lipscomb College (Nashville), began calling for equal time for the creation account. Creationists in Louisiana, Michigan, Washington State, Georgia, West Virginia, Montana, and Arkansas began to pick up on this strategy. Then in 1981 the governor of Arkansas signed Law 590, effectively requiring a "balanced treatment" of creation science and evolution science in the public schools. United States District Court Judge William R. Overton overturned Law 590 on the grounds that it was a clear violation of the Establishment Clause. In his decision Overton provided a detailed definition of science and wrote that creation science is not science. The court found that the law depended too much on the language in creationist literature. It also said that although speculations about life's origins can be a minor part of biology, the main thrust of evolutionary theory is what has happened *after* life originated; therefore, the charge that evolution is antireligious was unfounded.

The result in Arkansas quelled the "equal time movement" in other states.[129]

Edwards v. Aguillard (1987; Louisiana)

The Louisiana "Creation Act" stipulated that the teaching of evolution could only happen when accompanied by the teaching of creation science. The United States Supreme Court voted 7-2 that creationism and creation science were inherently religious teachings, not science. Since the Louisiana law advocated the belief that a supernatural God created humanity, the high court ruled, the result was an impermissible endorsement of religion, violating—you guessed it—the Establishment Clause.[130]

Webster v. New Lennox School District (1990; Illinois)

The New Lennox School District acted to prevent one of its teachers from teaching creation science. He sued, claiming his freedom of speech was being curtailed. The U.S. Seventh Circuit Court of Appeals decided that a school district could take such action to make sure the Establishment Clause was not being violated. It also ruled that the teacher had been performing religious advocacy, not using his free speech, and that his free-speech rights were not violated.[131]

Peloza v. Capistrano Unified School District (1994; California)

John Peloza, a teacher in the Capistrano district, charged that requiring him to teach evolution in his biology class violated his free-speech rights. He also claimed that being forced to teach evolution amounted to establishing (there's that word again) secular humanism as the state religion. The U.S. Ninth Circuit Court of Appeals rejected Peloza's argument, ruling that the school district had merely required a science teacher to teach science.[132]

Freiler v. Tangipahoa Parish Board of Education (1997; Louisiana)

The Tangipahoa Parish Board of Education in Louisiana had a policy that required teachers to read a disclaimer about evolution before teaching about it, with the stated goal of promoting critical thinking. The disclaimer read:

> . . . It is hereby recognized by the Tangipahoa Board of Education, that the lesson to be presented, regarding the origin of life and matter, is known as the Scientific Theory of Evolution and should be presented to inform students of the scientific concept and not intended to influence or dissuade the Biblical version of Creation or any other concept. It is further recognized by the Board of Education that it is the basic right and privilege of each student to form his/her own opinion and maintain beliefs taught by parents on this very important matter of the origin of life and matter. Students are urged to exercise critical thinking and gather all information possible and closely examine each alternative toward forming an opinion.

The U.S. District Court of the Eastern District of Louisiana rejected this policy because, the court said, it singled out evolution for the disclaimer and singled out the biblical concept of creation as a belief that was not to be discouraged.[133]

Rodney LeVake v. Independent School District 656 (2001; Minnesota)

LeVake, a high school biology teacher, petitioned his district for permission to teach evidence both for and against evolution. The district refused and LeVake sued. The Third Judicial District Court of Minnesota refused to hear the case, ruling that LeVake's free-speech rights did not override his responsibility to teach the curriculum and that the district had not practiced religious discrimination. Both the Minneapolis Supreme Court and U.S. Supreme Court declined to hear the appeals.[134]

Kansas Board of Education v. Itself (1999–2007)

This wasn't a court case, but in 1999 the Kansas Board of Education removed some controversial aspects of evolutionary theory from the state-mandated curriculum. The local and national press went into an uproar, accusing the board of backwardness, lack of common sense, and betraying science itself. In 2001, after three of its members were unseated, the board reinstated the teaching of the Big Bang and evolution, without any more restriction on teaching the theory.[135]

The Kansas board was far from out of the spotlight, however. In November 2005 it approved new public school science standards that cast doubt on the theory of macroevolution. The board voted 6-4 in what was considered a victory for Intelligent Design advocates. One board member who voted for the standards, John Bacon, said the move "gets rid of a lot of dogma that's being taught in the classroom today."[136] But in February 2007 the board would swing back the other way, and again by a 6-4 vote! It voted to repeal the science guidelines that questioned evolution, and called for its curriculum to reflect mainstream science views of evolution—once again a setback for the Intelligent Design movement.

> THE KANSAS BOARD WAS FAR FROM OUT OF THE SPOTLIGHT, HOWEVER. IN NOVEMBER 2005 IT APPROVED NEW PUBLIC SCHOOL SCIENCE STANDARDS THAT **CAST DOUBT ON THE THEORY OF MACROEVOLUTION.**

Ohio Board of Education v. Itself (2002–2006)

This is another episode that didn't go to court. In 2002, the Discovery Institute, an Intelligent Design think tank based in Seattle, suggested a model curriculum that included ID and advocated "teaching the controversy."

> **TEACHING THE CONTROVERSY:** The phrase has been linked with the Discovery Institute and refers to teaching both creation and evolution—from teaching Darwinism to teaching the arguments creationists bring against evolution.

The Ohio School Board partially adopted the standards in 2002 with the condition that those standards do "not mandate the teaching or testing of intelligent design." But in 2006 the state board reversed itself, voting 11-4 to delete the plan.[137]

Selman v. Cobb County School District (2004–2006; Georgia)

In 2002 the Cobb County School Board (Georgia) decided that all science textbooks must have a sticker with the following disclaimer:

> *This textbook contains material on evolution. Evolution is a theory, not a fact, regarding the origin of living things. This material should be approached with an open mind, studied carefully, and critically considered.*

Two years later Jeffrey Selman and two other parents sued to have the stickers removed. In 2005 Federal District Judge Clarence Cooper found that the "evolution warning" stickers violated the Establishment Clause because they were creationist in intent, that they claimed evolution was "only a theory," and that they didn't explain what "theory" meant. After some back-and-forth maneuvering in the appeals process, in 2006 the case was settled out of court in favor of Selman and the other plaintiffs. There are no longer such stickers on Cobb County textbooks.[138]

WHAT DO WE NOTICE ABOUT NEARLY ALL OF THE CASES? **IT'S NOT A REAL GREAT SCORECARD FOR CREATIONISM, CREATION SCIENCE, OR INTELLIGENT DESIGN** IN PUBLIC SCHOOL CLASSROOMS.

A Brief Recap of Case Law

What do we notice about nearly all of the cases above? It's not a real great scorecard for creationism, creation science, or Intelligent Design in public school classrooms.

Those holding those views have racked up a string of losses in the courts, the results greatly affecting what's being taught in public schools. Three basic strategies have been tried:

- *1925–1981 — From Scopes to Segraves: attempts to remove evolution theory and the teaching of evolutionism from the classrooms*

- *1970–1987 — From McLean to Edwards: attempts to gain equal time for the creationist perspective*

- *1987–present — From Webster to Selman: evolution portrayed as one among other scientific theories or as a philosophy of life/worldview*

And one more trial, even more recent, fit under that last bill. Things didn't go much better in what many people have called Scopes II, or "the second monkey trial" . . .

Kitzmiller v. Dover Area School District (2005; Pennsylvania)

After *Edwards v. Aguillard* (1987), the creationist movement was hurting. Phillip Johnson, a Berkeley law professor, rallied the troops and tried to get them to put aside differences and concentrate on something all could agree on: Intelligent Design. By 1990 the ID movement had launched the Discovery Institute, published the book *Of Pandas and People*, and had begun designing an academic curriculum.

In 2004 the Dover (Pennsylvania) Area School District, frustrated that God had repeatedly been cut out of public schools, decided to practice a little affirmative action for God. They put in place new Intelligent Design curriculum standards, chose *Of Pandas and People* as a supplemental biology text, and drafted a four-paragraph statement on ID that was to be read aloud to all students, inviting them to read *Pandas* if they so desired:

The Pennsylvania Academic Standards require students to learn about Darwin's theory of evolution and eventually to take a standardized test of which evolution is a part.

Because Darwin's Theory is a theory, it is still being tested as new evidence is discovered. The Theory is not a fact. Gaps in the Theory

IN 2004 THE DOVER (PENNSYLVANIA) AREA SCHOOL DISTRICT, FRUSTRATED THAT GOD HAD REPEATEDLY BEEN CUT OUT OF PUBLIC SCHOOLS, DECIDED TO PRACTICE A LITTLE AFFIRMATIVE ACTION FOR GOD.

exist for which there is no evidence. A theory is defined as a well-tested explanation that unifies a broad range of observations.

Intelligent design is an explanation of the origin of life that differs from Darwin's view. The reference book, Of Pandas and People *is available for students to see if they would like to explore this view in an effort to gain an understanding of what intelligent design actually involves.*

As is true with any theory, students are encouraged to keep an open mind. The school leaves the discussion of the origins of life to individual students and their families. As a standards-driven district, class instruction focuses upon preparing students to achieve proficiency on standards-based assessments.[139]

Dover's science teachers balked at reading the statement, so the school board sent its staff into the classrooms to do so. Soon the board had a lawsuit on its hands, one involving the issue of separation of church and state.

The case was brought to the U.S. District Court for the Middle District of Pennsylvania. A star-studded cast on both sides of the debate was about to give testimony.

Then several things happened that did not bode well for the Intelligent Design case.

- *Before the trial, some of the biggest names on the ID side (William Dembski, Steven Meyer, and Warren Nord) decided, for complex reasons, that they would not testify.*

- *During the trial, the expert witnesses who represented evolution were persuasive. Kenneth R. Miller (referenced in chapter 3 under the Theistic Evolution section), a witness for the plaintiffs, said that Judge John E. Jones III "took notes like a desperate grad student throughout the trial." Miller wrote that, as he gave his testimony, he observed:*

[Jones] followed intently as I showed the exact point where primate chromosomes 12 and 13 had fused in one of our ancestors to produce human chromosome number 2. He noted glaring errors of molecular biology in Of Pandas and People, and laughed as Berkeley paleontology professor Kevin Padian pointed out the incredible misrepresentations of fossils in the same

book. His eyes opened wide as Professor Barbara Forrest from Southeastern Louisiana University showed how Of Pandas and People *had been fashioned from an earlier, overtly creationist book. The publishers had simply run the text through a word processor that changed each occurrence of "Creator" to "designer," and "creation" to "intelligent design."[140]*

- *Then, just as closing arguments were being made, the people of Dover voted to replace every one of the eight board members who had chosen to introduce ID.*

Six weeks later, in late December 2005, Jones gave his verdict. It wasn't a good one for Intelligent Design. Jones, a churchgoer and a conservative Republican appointed by President George W. Bush, observed that even though the ID group had claimed it had no religious motivation or agenda, it had severely compromised its testimony by previous writings and actions. Although this was the first time a federal court had dealt with ID specifically, *Dover* was a replay of the major issues that had come up in previous creationist cases. Jones ruled that ID is religion and not science, that ID does not belong in a science classroom, and that teaching ID in public schools is a violation of the Establishment Clause.[141]

GORILLA NATION?

Christian objections to Darwinism being taught in public schools is an ongoing hot topic. However, efforts to prevent the teaching of evolution, to insert creationism or Intelligent Design into the teaching materials, to create some equal time, and to offer some relatively bland disclaimers regarding evolution have all run smack into the brick wall of the Establishment Clause, at least as it's defined by the courts. Together, the cases have all pointed in the same direction: toward a legal consensus that Creationism (Young Earth and Old Earth) and Intelligent Design are religious beliefs and not science. So are the public courts opting for "gorillas" (Darwin) and leaving little room for God in the equation?

Even though Intelligent Design is a powerful instinctive argument, in the courts it's gasping for air. What are the implications in the wider culture?

- *Whether it is science or not, ID took a big hit in the Dover case when it portrayed itself as nonreligious.*

- The court case cost the Dover Area School Board about $2 million. School districts wanting to implement ID standards might find the potential price tag of future lawsuits too hefty.

- The legal precedent could result in further restrictions on Christian voices in the public schools.

- Social pressure on American schoolchildren to accept the worldview of naturalism (and thus, Naturalistic Evolution) could increase because evolution can easily be presented in a way that excludes God and makes faith in the Bible look unintelligent.

In this environment, as believers we need to think through two things. First, the Establishment Clause. Are we OK with the government not having a declared state religion, but at the same time allowing for the free exercise of all religions? I agree it's not good to cave in to a secularist mind-set of a strict wall of separation between church and state. That attitude only leads to badly misconstruing the Establishment Clause; it leads to abuses of religious freedom and free speech; and it logically concludes with the establishment of secularism as the state religion and banishing open religious expression from the public square. The absolute, strict wall of separation is discriminatory and unacceptable. On the other hand, we don't want to overreact and try to push the pendulum back to some form of control of the state by religion.

Second, worldviews. In our increasingly pluralistic culture, it's all the more important to teach Christian parents and students what's at stake regarding worldviews, to uphold the white-hot core of Christian faith, and to honestly teach the positives and difficulties of the various approaches to the creation/evolution controversy.

The bottom line—no matter where you come down on the creation/evolution debate—is to seek to act wisely, effectively, and persuasively for the gospel.

15 APE OR ANGEL?

Is man an ape or an angel?
Now I am on the side of the angels.
—BENJAMIN DISRAELI, BRITISH STATESMAN AND PRIME
MINISTER (1804-1881)

Who take their manners from the Ape,
Their habits from the Bear,
Indulge the loud unseemly jape,
And never brush their hair.
—HILAIRE BELLOC, FRENCH-BORN POET AND WRITER
(1870-1953)

In the early 1500s, Portuguese sailors visiting the island of Mauritius in the Indian Ocean discovered a strange flightless bird. The sailors named them dodos because the birds walked right up to hunters, who then clubbed them to death and ate them. They soon went extinct.

Centuries later, in his 2006 documentary *A Flock of Dodos*, evolutionary biologist Randy Olson made dodo birds a metaphor for two kinds of people: the public, who in large numbers reject Darwinian evolution; and the scientific community, which in its arrogance and condescension has failed to teach evolutionary theory convincingly.[142]

> LIKE YOU, I'VE BEEN CONFUSED. LIKE YOU, I'VE BUSTED MY BRAIN TRYING TO FIGURE THESE THINGS OUT.

As I've studied the creation/evolution controversy, I've found myself relating to those dodo birds. I've often felt as though I was aimless, wandering, about to be clubbed! Such lofty subject matter! Such complicated ideas! Such massive literature! How can anybody wrap his or her mind around it?

That's one of the big reasons I've written this book. Like you, I've been confused. Like you, I've busted my brain trying to figure these things out. (Oh, you haven't? Good for you!) Maybe this last chapter will help you see where I'm coming from, why I'm not all fire-and-brimstone about my position, why for the most part I refuse to put down those who disagree with me, and why I've written some of the things I have.

MISSION: CHIMPOSSIBLE

The Chimpossible mission of this book, which I have chosen to accept, is to try to show how Young Earth Creationism, Old Earth Creationism, Intelligent Design, and Trinitarian Theistic Evolution all operate within the basic outline of the biblical worldview (God as creator, who has authority over his world and can act in it). And I've sought to show that these views do not conflict with historic orthodox Christianity (what Christians have held most important through the centuries). But I have also sought to show that they clash on their interpretations of science and on the best way to read the first chapters of the Bible.

Sincere, well-meaning, reasonable people may disagree, and disagree strongly, on these issues. Wait—I've had ongoing disagreements with myself on this! In fact, at one time or another in my life, I've held each of the five positions mentioned in this book.

So no matter where you come down in the Late Great Ape Debate, try to remember:

- *That people are not necessarily set in stone on these questions. They may waver, they may be inconsistent, they may swing from one position to the next. These questions have tested the best of minds. Realize that, for the most part, people are doing the best they can with what they've got.*

- *That these are not primary issues (such as the basic truths of God, Jesus, the Holy Spirit, the Bible, and salvation) but instead are pious opinions about secondary matters (such as how we try to relate faith and reason, or faith and science). For a refresher on these things, if needed, see chapter 2.*

- *That part of following Jesus is extending fair-mindedness and charity to those with whom we disagree. Therefore, try to go very light on sarcasm or attributing bad motives to people who don't share your opinion on the somewhat difficult issue of how we all got here to begin with. It might be hard because you feel so strongly about your position, but do it anyway.*

- *That it's good to value your brothers and sisters who hold the other three biblical worldview positions that you don't. It's also a good mental exercise to try to understand why they believe as they do. You might never find out, but it's a good exercise anyway.*

What I really want is to encourage people to bring their A-game in both faith and science to these questions. In doing so, I hope to get people more excited about God and his creation, more excited about Jesus, more passionate about sharing the gospel in our skeptical and pluralistic culture, and more effective in doing so.

Maybe you've been to Disneyland. As a kid, one of my favorite rides there was Autopia, where, once you were able to stretch yourself up to about 44 inches tall, you could drive your own putt-putt car. Now, I give you a brief circuit of my own creation/evolution journey, a ride that we will call . . .

CHIMPTOPIA

Before I became a Christian, I was very close to holding to the viewpoint that we have called Naturalistic Evolution. I wasn't sure if I believed in God, and whatever I might have believed about him—if he existed at all—was that he was unfriendly, unapproachable, remote from human affairs.

Then, at a youth rally, I heard the gospel for the first time. What an amazing message! I became a Christian and began, clumsily but self-consciously, to follow Jesus. I connected with Christian fellowship and started reading the Bible.

As a new Christian, I leaned toward the view I was taught: a literal interpretation of the first chapters of Genesis. But a "presto" creation complete with "the appearance of age" was problematic to me. And despite the fact that flood narratives are in the stories that many peoples and cultures tell of their past, a worldwide flood similarly seemed incredible to me. Early in my spiritual journey I asked my dad, a petroleum geologist for Shell Oil, what he thought. He said that if there had been a flood like that described in Genesis 6–8, massive mud deposits should be easy to find. But, by his thinking and study, and that of other scientists as well, there were no such deposits. These kinds of thoughts began to work openings in my mind for Old Earth Creationism.

The Old Earth view freed me from the 4004 BC printed in the margin of my Bible. That date was just a note, a human interpretation, not God's Word itself! Old Earth Creationism was able to absorb physical evidence from astronomy, geology, paleontology, and archaeology. There was now room, as I saw it, for ancient civilizations prior to 4000 BC; cavemen and their paintings; several ice ages; saber-toothed tigers, woolly mammoths, and giant sloths; continents smashing together and being torn asunder through plate tectonics; dinosaurs; an immense universe and deep time.

So I had made the shift to Old Earth. That made it easier for me to later look into what some have called the "big tent" of ideas encompassed by Intelligent Design and Trinitarian Theistic Evolution.

UNDER THE BIG TOP

Like many people, I've been fascinated by Intelligent Design's "big tent" approach. Regarding biblical texts and theology, ID takes the stance of leaving a remarkable amount of space for disagreement and debate.

Intelligent Design is noncommittal on the Big Bang and deep time; it is noncommittal on whether to translate the Hebrew word *yom* as "day" or "era." And for many, it is even noncommittal on the identity of the intelligent designer! But you'll often hear something like this from people in the movement, most of whom are believing Christians: "Intelligent Design doesn't speculate who the intelligent designer is, but in my opinion as a Christian, the intelligent designer is the God of the Bible."

Intelligent Design proponents want to shift the discussion from Bible texts and theology to worldviews, philosophy, and science.

Regarding worldviews: Intelligent Design insists that you can never just forget about the importance of worldviews; they must always be part of the picture.

Regarding philosophy: Intelligent Design extensively employs the apparent

> YOU'LL OFTEN HEAR "INTELLIGENT DESIGN DOESN'T SPECULATE WHO THE INTELLIGENT DESIGNER IS, BUT IN MY OPINION AS A CHRISTIAN, THE INTELLIGENT DESIGNER IS THE GOD OF THE BIBLE."

design and purpose of living organisms and biological systems. It points to the idea of a finely tuned universe to support teleological arguments (argument from design) for the existence of God (oops, I meant the intelligent designer!).

Regarding science: Intelligent Design takes a nuanced approach. Recently I had a fascinating dinner conversation with one of the leading Intelligent Design proponents, a man with a PhD in microbiology who was part of a team that discovered a new species of pocket gopher in Texas.

We talked about worldviews, Trinitarian Theistic Evolution, microevolution and macroevolution, how some species can naturally differentiate into new species, Intelligent Design's "big tent," whether resurrection from the dead or the parting of the Red Sea can be verified through science, the evidences for divine creativity and power in the effects and appearances of different classes of living beings, evolutionary biologist Steven Jay Gould's ideas that Darwinian evolution is "directionless" (and that if you "rewound the clock" evolution could have yielded entirely different results), and the 2005 Dover Trial.

It was amazing we had time to eat! It would have been fun to cover everything, but we ran out of time. If we'd had the better part of the night, I expect we may have talked about a bunch of other things, like the very rare conditions that make complex life possible (the anthropic principle), the irreducible complexity of the bacterial flagellum, the Cambrian explosion (in which many scientists say all families of biological life appeared), the possible-but-as-yet undiscovered functions of junk DNA (and the presumptuousness in calling it junk when it hasn't been fully studied), and lots more.

> WHETHER THE EARTH EXPERIENCES GLOBAL WARMING, GLOBAL COOLING, ASTEROID IMPACTS, DINOSAUR DIE-OFFS, EVIL LEADERS COMING TO POWER, WARS, OR ECONOMIC COLLAPSES, **GOD IS STILL SOVEREIGN.**

Later, I viewed a pro-Intelligent Design DVD (2007 release) that this friend gave me. The DVD's second session begins with a counterargument for nearly every major claim evolutionists (neo-Darwinians) put forth. But in the fourth and last session the point is made that Intelligent Design uses science, and is scientific, but "is not yet science" and "more time is needed" for it to become an actual scientific theory.[143] Watching the DVD surprised me because in all the literature I had read by Intelligent Design proponents, the claim had been made that the ID movement *is* science. I take from this that the 2005 Dover Trial and its aftermath have caused some rethinking of this positioning in the ID camp. That's OK. As a movement Intelligent Design is only a couple of decades old. But I am still amazed at how big Intelligent Design's "big tent" really is.

GOD OR GORILLAS—IS THAT THE QUESTION?

"God or Gorillas (the latter being a metaphor for evolution)?" This is only one of the questions swirling around the Late Great Ape Debate. As we work our way through these questions, whatever else we do, we should agree on the following things, based on a broad understanding of the biblical worldview.

No matter how God created the universe, it's a magnificent job! So all who believe in God believe in an intelligent designer (turn again to Romans 1:19, 20).

Whether God used a Big Bang and billions of years or a short week of time to create the world, he's still the "first cause." If the Big Bang happened as naturalistic scientists describe it, it's always a fair question to ask, "Well then, where did the Big Bang come from?" Teaching God as the first cause doesn't tell us everything about God, but it does give us some idea of his incredible creative power.

No matter what means God uses to accomplish his purposes, whether we understand how he's doing what he's doing or not, God takes everything that happens and steers it, directs it, and moves it providentially toward his greater will. Whether the earth experiences global warming, global cooling, asteroid impacts, dinosaur die-offs, evil leaders coming to power, wars, or economic collapses, God is still sovereign.

THEREFORE, WHEREVER AND WHENEVER GENETIC CHANGES HAVE HAPPENED, **IT'S ARROGANT FOR HUMANS TO PROCLAIM THAT GOD COULDN'T HAVE BEEN INVOLVED AT ALL.**

However useful science is in giving us a better understanding of how the natural world works, it can't arbitrarily and with finality exclude God or his activity in the natural world.

The field of genetics is strongly dependent on statistical analysis. But statistics, while helpful, can't tell the whole story about every particular case. Therefore, wherever and whenever genetic changes have happened, whether by random mutation or the direct hand of God (or both!), it's arrogant for humans to proclaim that God couldn't have been involved at all. If neo-Darwinian macroevolution did happen, I believe it happened under the watch of the Trinity—God the Father, God the Son, and God the Holy Spirit. To be faithful to the biblical worldview, you have to believe in miracles. Thus, any theory of Theistic Evolution that excludes miracles and makes God aloof and deistic (see chapter 1 for deism) is not the biblical worldview and excludes the gospel.

God designed and loves each of us—read Psalm 139:13-16 and 1 John 3:1; 4:16, among others, for these two ideas! His love never fails, even if our genes aren't perfect, even if we have genetic hiccups, even if we're not among "the beautiful people," as society defines them for us.

However you resolve the creation/evolution debate for yourself, the main question needs to be: Which worldview? The biblical worldview of Jesus? Or some other?

WHAT TO TEACH THE CHILDREN

My wife and I haven't had a single approach to the question of how to teach our children about creation and evolution. My own views have been developing over time; children themselves go through their own stages of cognitive development; and individual children are different. I don't have *the* answer for everybody. I can only tell you what our family did.

We homeschooled our children through middle school (truthfully, my wife did most of it). We loved doing educational things with them, reading them to bed, going to the library. We tried to give them a stimulating environment and protect them from harmful influences. For most of that time we didn't have TV, but we provided plenty of other more interactive opportunities.

At first, my wife and I decided to protect our kids from evolution because we thought it might confuse them and possibly harm their young faith. We took them to church and to the zoo, but we hid the Time-Life books on evolution. Later, we lightened up. People are going to be exposed to evolution no matter what. Might as well make the best of it.

When they were in middle school, here's what we told our children: When God created the world, he put a lot of puzzles in it. (Jesus also gave us puzzles when he told parables, and he told a lot of them.) Some puzzles are easy and some are very hard. God also gave us minds and he wants us to use them. And he made us so our minds want to work on those puzzles! Our job, then, is to search the Scriptures, love God with our hearts, do the science, and work the puzzles out as best we can with our minds.

We also tried to instill in our children values like the dignity and worth of each individual—based upon being created in the image of God, following Jesus, honoring the Word of God (the Bible), and learning as much as you can.

What do I recommend today? When the day comes that you have children, and they're young, take them outdoors (hikes, camping, the zoo, whatever) and teach them to catch the wonder of God's amazing, magnificent creation. Teach the stories in the Bible just as they are. Let them relive the mighty acts God did for his people.

Teach about Jesus, what he was like, the things he did. Help them fall in love with the Jesus-who-is-alive-now. Let's not mess the picture up by presenting Jesus as some musty long-ago-remote-guy-then. Pray with them and rejoice with them when God answers prayer.

Then, when they're in middle school or high school (different children are ready at different ages), start teaching them the basic worldviews and what makes the biblical worldview so totally unique and good compared to the alternatives. Teach them not to be afraid of science, but to get excited about it. And be sure to teach them about the scope, limits, and methods of the Bible and science—but that God is in no way limited in any act—and that vibrant faith and science aren't in essential conflict.

> TEACH THEM THE BASIC WORLD-VIEWS AND WHAT MAKES THE BIBLICAL WORLDVIEW SO TOTALLY UNIQUE AND GOOD COMPARED TO THE ALTERNATIVES.

As a final note on this, my wife and I aren't exactly on the same page regarding creation and evolution. Like many people, the watchmaker arguments (like the intricacy of the eye and many other examples) powerfully move my wife to worship our creator. To this I say amen! Nature surely exists to bring glory to God. He is a marvelous intelligent designer.

LIVING HIGHER THAN THE APES

Here is what I've attempted to maintain from start to end in this book: That we hold up a high view of Scripture and a high respect for science. As I see it, the most important battle being fought every day is over worldviews. Too often Christians get wrapped up in nonessentials and give up too much essential gospel turf. We need to learn when a worldview is biblical and when it is not, when the core of Christian faith is being attacked and when it is not.

If we want to impact our culture with the gospel, we need to quickly and accurately recognize when scientists are wearing their science hats and when they're wearing their personal worldview opinions hats—and teach our children to do the same. We also need to quickly and accurately recognize when Christians are giving us good, solid doctrine and (alternately) when they are weighing down the gospel with nonessential add-ons—and we need to teach our children to do the same. This is a stewardship issue. It is a gospel issue. It is a missionary issue. If we fail on this count, Christians will become increasingly marginalized in our own culture.

Lately I've heard Christians say things like, "I can't be bothered with this whole creation/evolution thing. To me, it doesn't matter." Maybe they're thinking, "Who's to say who's right? It's all just one person's interpretation over another." Maybe they feel it's an unnecessary distraction and that we should just get out there and be feeding the poor. (Which we should!) Maybe they're too harried and harassed by life's responsibilities. Maybe they've been swamped by information overload. Maybe, along with nineteenth-century poet John Keats, they believe that this "cold philosophy . . . will clip an Angel's wings."[144]

I say it matters because people are made in God's image for a relationship with him through Christ. It matters because Jesus said to love God with our hearts and souls and strength and minds (Matthew 22:37; Mark 12:30), all of which is what it means to be made in God's image. And it matters because, in our wider culture, God deserves not just a better reputation, but fame, praise, and glory.

Notes

A DAY AT THE MUSEUM

1. Brandon Ortiz, "New Kentucky Museum Promotes Literal Biblical View," *Lexington Herald-Leader*, June 2, 2007, online at www.venturacountystar.com/news/2007/jun/02/no-headline—le1fccreationmus02/ (accessed March 23, 2008).

2. From Chapter 2 of Walden, found at the University of Virginia American Studies website http://xroads.virginia.edu-/-Hyper/WALDEN/hdt02.html (accessed May 8, 2007).

CULT OF THE HAIRY APE

3. From Henrietta A. Huxley, comp., *Aphorisms and Reflections* (London: Macmillan, 1907), Reflection #229; and *The Columbia World of Quotations* (New York: Columbia University Press, 1996), found at www.bartleby.com/66/18/30018.html (accessed December 20, 2007).

4. Deism accepts a creator-God, but denies specific Christian truth claims. Deism says you can know God through reason alone. While many deists believe God is absolutely aloof from the world he has created, others, like Benjamin Franklin and Thomas Jefferson (whose God was influenced by Jewish and Christian tradition), believe that the deistic God can be petitioned and that he will participate in human affairs.

5. David L. George, ed., *The Family Book of Best Loved Poems* (New York: Doubleday & Company, 1952), from "Evolution" (1.111-112), by Langdon Smith (1858-1908), U.S. poet. See *The Columbia World of Quotations* (New York: Columbia University Press, 1996); found at www.bartleby.com/66/40/54340.html (accessed December 21, 2007).

6. Alex Johnson, MSNBC reporter, "Lessons Learned from Monkeying with History," www.msnbc.msn.com/id/8564480 (accessed December 21, 2007).

7. Archival photos at "Anti-Evolution League–The Conflict-Hell & the High School" at www.assumption.edu/ahc/scopes/antievolutionleague.jpg (accessed December 21, 2007).

8. PBS website, "American Experience: Monkey Trial," at www.pbs.org/wgbh/amex/monkeytrial/peopleevents/e_trial.html (accessed December 21, 2007; in all notations afterward: *PBS Monkey*).

9. Trial transcripts at Andy Bradbury's Neuro-Linguistic Programming website at www.bradburyac.mistral.co.uk/tenness2.html (accessed December 21, 2007). See also Doug Linder's University of Missouri-Kansas City School of Law "Scopes Trial Home Page" at www.law.umkc.edu/faculty/projects/ftrials/scopes/scopes.htm (in all notations afterward: *UMKCSL*; accessed December 21, 2007).

10. UMKCSL.

11. See Mencken's reports of "The Monkey Trial" on UMKCSL at www.law.umkc .edu/faculty/projects/ftrials/scopes/menk.htm (accessed December 27, 2007).

12. Ibid.

13. Ibid.

14. See "gallery" at PBS Monkey (accessed September 12, 2007).

15. UMKCSL, Mencken's reports of the trial.

16. See the University of California Museum of Paleontology website article "Thomas Henry Huxley (1825-1895)" at www.ucmp.berkeley.edu/history/thuxley.html (accessed December 28, 2007). See also the ScienceWeek website, "On Darwin and Huxley" at http://scienceweek.com/2004/sa040507-3.htm (accessed September 12, 2007).

17. PBS Monkey (accessed December 28, 2007).

VERY APE AND VERY NICE

18. See the Weissmuller Family genealogy webpage at www.codap.com/weissmuller/ tarzan.htm (accessed September 29, 2007).

19. A phrase made famous in Carl Sagan's TV show "Cosmos," see http:// en.wikipedia.org/wiki/Cosmos:_A_Personal_Voyage (accessed October 2, 2007).

20. For an entertaining read on this, see John Derbyshire, "Teaching Science: The president is wrong on Intelligent Design," found at http://nationalreview.com/scrdipt/ printpage.p?ref=/derbyshire/derbyshire200509300823.asp (accessed August 30, 2005).

21. For a lively scientific debate, see (a) Clive Cookson, "Chimp and Human DNA is 96% Identical," The Financial Times online at http://news.ft.com/cms/s/43445278-1a44-11da-b279-00000e2511c8.html (September 1, 2005); (b) Steven Sternberg, "Humans, Chimps Almost a Match," USA *Today* (September 1, 2005); (c) John Pickrell, "Chimpanzees Shed Light on the Evolution of Human Senses" (published March 19, 2004), found on the Human Genome website at http://genome.wellcome .ac.uk/doc_WTD020881.html (accessed May 22, 2007); (d) Elizabeth Pennisi, "Jumbled DNA Separates Chimps and Humans," which disputes the "98.5% identical" assertion with recent genome studies in *Science* 298:719 (October 25, 2002); (e) Bob Holmes, "Chromosomes Reveal Surprise Human-Chimp Differences," which reports on a Japanese study that revises the 98.5 percent similarity to 83 percent based upon comparing the amino acid production of chromosome 22 in chimps with its chromosome 21 human counterpart, found on the New Scientist website at www .newscientist.com/article.ns?id=5044 (accessed May 22, 2007).

TAKIN' CARE OF (MONKEY) BUSINESS

22. Some examples: David Van Biema, "Reconciling God and Science: Genome mapper Francis Collins is also an evangelical Christian. His new book says that's not

a contradiction," *Time Magazine* (July 17, 2006). See also Jim Vadehei's poison-pill debate question for the Republican presidential candidates, "Do you believe in evolution?" See page 18 of the debate transcript on the *New York Times* website at www.nytimes.com/2007/05/03/us/politics/04transcript.html?ex=1189828800&en=492a506aa38a7c1e&ei=5070 (accessed September 12, 2007). See also President Bush's 2005 response to teaching Intelligent Design in public schools: "Both sides ought to be properly taught . . . so people can understand what the debate is about." See also John Derbyshire, "Teaching Science: the president is wrong on Intelligent Design" on *National Review Online* at www.nationalreview.com/derbyshire/derbyshire200508300823.asp (August 30, 2005); and Peter Baker and Peter Slevin, "Bush Remarks on 'Intelligent Design' Theory Fuel Debate," *Washington Post* (August 3, 2005. See also Brian Cabell, "Kansas School Board's Ruling Angers Science Community" (August 12, 1999) on the Kansas Board of Education's efforts to outlaw or diminish the teaching of evolution in public schools, found on CNN's website at www.cnn.com/US/9908/12/kansas.evolution.flap (accessed September 12, 2007). See also Claudia Wallis, "Evolution Wars," *Time* Magazine (August 15, 2005; in all notations afterward: *Wallis*, p. 28).

23. David Dobbs in *Charles Darwin, Alexander Agassiz*, and the *Meaning of Coral* (Pantheon, 2005), quoted in a book review by Anthony Day, "A Family Grudge Against Darwinism," *Los Angeles Times* (January 3, 2005), p. E6.

24. A typical treatment of this subject is Steven Austin, *Grand Canyon: Monument to Catastrophe* (Santee, CA: Institute for Creation Research, 1995).

25. An entire BBC website is dedicated to this famous hoax at http://news.bbc .co.uk/1/shared/spl/hi/sci_nat/03/piltdown_man/html/default.stm (9/27/2007).

26. Wallis, p. 35.

27. Ibid.

28. See the report of a 2007 Gallup Poll on the topic at www.usatoday.com/news/politics/2007-06-07-evolution-poll-results_N.htm?csp=34 (accessed October 1, 2007).

29. Hugh Ross, *The Creator and the Cosmos: How the Greatest Scientific Discoveries of the Century Reveal God* (Colorado Springs, CO: NavPress, 1993) p. 15.

30. "The gap" theory was first widely spread in the 1909 edition of the immensely influential *Scofield Reference Bible*.

31. Greg Neyman, "Old Earth Creation Science: Noah's Flood" (May 29, 2003) on the Answers in Creation website at www.answersincreation.org/flood.htm (accessed October 1, 2007).

32. According to the Creation Report of the 71st Assembly of the orthodox Presbyterian Church (2004), "the gap" theory became prominent among pre-World War II fundamentalists after having been promoted in the *Scofield Reference Bible*. It continues to be held by some. See www.opc.org/GA/CreationReport.pdf (accessed February 9, 2008).

33. See Rich Deem, "The 'Gap' Creation Model", on the God and Science website at www.godandscience.org/apologetics/gap.html (accessed February 9, 2008).

34. See Hugh Ross' Reasons To Believe website at www.reasons.org (in all notations afterward: *Reasons*; accessed September 3, 2005).

35. Other well-known evangelicals holding this position are John Ankerberg, Charles Colson, William Laine Craig, Norman Geisler, Hank Hanegraff, Jack Hayford, Greg Kouki, Mark Noll, Nancy Pearcey, Vern Poythress, and Lee Strobel. See the "notable leaders" link at the Reasons website (accessed June 4, 2007).

36. See Francisco J. Ayala, *Darwin's Gift to Science and Religion* (Washington, D.C.: Joseph Henry Press, 2007), p. 23 and endnote 18 for chapter 2. (In all notations afterward: *Ayala*.)

37. Ibid., p. 23-24 and footnote 19 for chapter 2.

38. Ibid., p. 26. Ayala's brief history of Intelligent Design arguments before Darwin's work is very helpful; see pp. 23-26.

39. Ibid., p. 26.

40. Paley's *Natural Theology* is available to read online. See the University of California Museum of Paleontology website at www.ucmp.berkeley.edu/history/paley .html (accessed May 19, 2007).

41. See Steven C. Meyer's Discovery Institute webpage. The Institute's catchphrase is "a non-profit, non-partisan, public policy think tank . . . dealing with national and international affairs." Discovery's website is at www.discovery.org (accessed May 20, 2007; in all notations afterward: *Discovery*).

42. Wallis, p. 35.

43. For example, Phillip E. Johnson's *The Wedge of Truth: Splitting the Foundations of Naturalism* (Downer's Grove: InterVarsity Press, 2002).

44. Discovery (accessed May 28, 2007). See also *Redeeming Darwin: The Intelligent Design Controversy*, a booklet, DVD, and website developed by Probe Ministries and EvanTell (Richardson, TX: Probe Ministries and Dallas, TX: EvanTell, 2007).

45. A phrase coined by Howard J. Van Till. See his essay in J. P. Moreland & John Mark Reynolds, editors, *Three Views on Creation and Evolution* (Grand Rapids: Zondervan, 1999; rev. ed. 2004).

46. Ayala, pp. 163-164. Another excellent resource on the history is George Marsden, *The Soul of the American University: From Protestant Establishment to Established Unbelief* (New York: Oxford University Press, 1994).

47. From Pope John Paul II's speech (October 22, 1996), found on the Catholic Information Network at www.cin.org/jp2evolu.html (accessed March 19, 2008).

48. Wallis, p. 34.

49. Kenneth R. Miller, *Finding Darwin's God: A Scientist's Search for Common Ground Between God and Evolution* (New York: HarperCollins, 1999, 2007). (In all notations afterward: *Miller*.)

50. A phrase from Alfred, Lord Tennyson, *In Memoriam* A.H.H. (1850), canto lvi. Found in *Oxford*, p. 536 #29.

51. Found on Amazon.com at www.amazon.com/exec/obidos/tg/detail/-/0393315703/103-336466-0384612?v=glance (accessed March 21, 2008).

52. Richard Dawkins, *River Out of Eden* (New York: HarperCollins, 1992), p. 133; quoted in Ayala, p. 173.

53. See Charlie Rose's video interview of E.O. Wilson and James Watson at http://video.google.com/videoplay?docid=-6927851714963534233&q=james+watson (accessed September 17, 2006).

54. Found at the National Council for Science Education website, www.ncseweb.org/resources/articles/8954_nabt_statement_on_evolution_ev_5_21_1998_asp (accessed September 3, 2005). The 1995 statement was corrected, after vigorous debate, in 1998.

55. Richard Dawkins, *The God Delusion* (Boston: Houghton Mifflin, 2006), quote from first chapter found on Richard Dawkins' website at richarddawkins.net/godDelusion (accessed September 10, 2007).

56. Larry Arnhart, "Evolution and Ethics," *Books & Culture* (November-December 1999), pp. 36-39.

TROLLING WITH TROGLODYTES

57. Here I'd like to give a plug to the American Scientific Affiliation, a model of civility, which counts among its members young and old earth creationists as well as proponents of Intelligent Design and Theistic Evolution. Its website is http://asa3.org (accessed March 21, 2008).

58. Associated Press, "Famous Atheist Now Believes in God: One of World's Leading Atheists Now Believes in God, More or Less, Based on Scientific Evidence" (December 9, 2004), reported by ABC News and found at http://abcnews.go.com/US/wireStory?id=315976 (accessed August 3, 2005).

59. Ibid.

60. See Charles Colson's Breakpoint radio commentary transcript (January 11, 2005) at www.queenofpeace.ca/Flew.htm (accessed August 3, 2005).

THE MISSING LINK

61. See Romans 14:1-23; 1 Corinthians 8:1-13; 10:14-33.

THE REVOLUTION OF EVOLUTION

62. For a partial list of Scriptures purportedly supporting a literal three-tiered universe, see Edward T. Babinski's website www.talkorigins.org/faqs/ce/2/part4.html (accessed September 14, 2007). See also Job 9:6; 26:7; 38–41; Psalm 19:4-6; 104:1-9; and Ecclesiastes 1:5.

63. For the church fathers, see Edward T. Babinski's "Did the Authors of the Bible Assume the Earth was Flat?" at http://edwardtbabinski.us/tektonics/flat_earth_bible .html (accessed September 14, 2007).

64. See "Papal Condemnation (Sentence) of Galileo, June 22, 1633" by following the "famous trials" and "Galileo" links on UMKCSL's website at www.law.umkc.edu/ faculty/projects/ftrials/galileo/condemnation.html (accessed September 14, 2007).

65. For dates having to do with Galileo's rehabilitation by the Catholic Church, see http://en.wikipedia.org/wiki/Galileo_Galilei (accessed September 15, 2007).

66. See Doug Linder, "Bishop James Ussher Sets the Date for Creation" (2004) by following the "famous trials" and "Ussher" links on UMKCSL's website at www.law .umkc.edu/faculty/projects/ftrials/scopes/ussher.html (accessed September 13, 2007).

67. See Simon Winchester, *The Map That Changed the World: William Smith and the Birth of Modern Geology* (New York: Harper Collins, 2001).

68. Francis S. Collins, *The Language of God: A Scientist Presents Evidence for Belief* (New York: Free Press, 2006), pp. 93-96. (In all notations afterward: *Collins*.)

69. Ayala, pp. 84-88.

70. Ayala, p. 95.

71. Here are the purported fossil remains that Ayala lists: Sahelanthropus (from 6–7 million years ago, or "mya"), Ardipithecus (4.4 mya), Australopithecus (3–4 mya), Homo habilis (1.5-2 mya), all originating in Africa. Homo erectus (1.8 mya) began in Africa and migrated to Europe, Asia, Indonesia, China, and the Middle East. Homo ergaster, Homo antecessor and Homo heidelbergensis (from 500,000 to 1.8 mya), originating in Africa and migrating into Europe and Asia; Homo sapiens (from 400,000 years ago); Homo neanderthalensis (200,000–30,000 years ago); and Homo sapiens (about 100,000 years ago).

72. Collins, summarizing pages 100-107.

73. Collins, p. 104.

74. Collins, p. 131.

75. Collins, pp. 125-126.

76. Collins, p. 126, puts the date at 100,000 to 140,000 years ago. See also Spencer Wells, *Deep Ancestry: Inside the Geographic Project* (Washington, D.C.: National Geographic, 2006), pp. 159-160.

77. Collins, pp. 137-141.

78. Collins, pp. 128-129. Collins does more with human-mouse and human-chimpanzee genome comparisons on pp. 133-141.

79. Quoted in John Darnton, "The Devolution of a Believer," *Los Angeles Times* (September 19, 2005) p. B13.

80. Ibid.

81. Collins, pp. 140-141.

A SERIOUS APE

82. Henry M. Morris, *Scientific Creationism* (Green River, OR: Master Books, 1974) p. 255.

83. Institute of Creation Research, "What is the Purpose of Creation Ministry?" *Back to Genesis Report No. 78* (June 1995).

84. Article found in Spencer Baynes and W. Robert Smith, eds., *Encyclopedia Britannica*, vols. 25-29 (Akron, OH: The Werner Company, 1907, American supplement published 1905) p. 659; digitized June 27, 2007 by the University of Virginia.

85. For a typical example, see "How Do We Know the Bible Is True?" on the Christian Answers website at www.christiananswers.net/q-eden/edn-t003.html (accessed March 12, 2008).

86. Stephen Jay Gould, "Non-Overlapping Magisteria," *Natural History* (March 1997) pp. 16ff.

SURRENDER MONKEYS

87. John S. Spong, "A Call for a New Reformation" in *The Voice* (May 1998); found on the website of the Episcopal Diocese of Newark at www.dioceseofnewark.org/vox20598.html (accessed September 16, 2007).

88. The five quotes that follow in this section are all from "A Call for a New Reformation," by John S. Spong.

89. Spong's version of Christian "post-modernism" (or postmodernism) is not the only one. Some versions do a good job of recasting the gospel in our contemporary culture. Others, including Spong's, are complete sellouts.

OH, GIVE ME A HOME WHERE THE DINOSAURS ROAM

90. Ashley Powers, "Adam, Eve and T-Rex," *Los Angeles Times* (August 27, 2005), p. A1. The quote is from Pastor Robert Darwin Chiles.

91. www.crosswalk.com's Bible concordance comments on *miym:* "Groups of living organisms belong in the same created 'kind' if they have descended from the same ancestral gene pool. This does not preclude new species because this represents a partitioning of the original gene pool. . . . A new species could arise when a population is isolated and inbreeding occurs. By this definition a new species is not a new 'kind' but a further partitioning of an existing 'kind.'" Found at http://bible.crosswalk.com/Lexicons/Hebrew/heb.cgi?number=04327&version=kjv (accessed September 19, 2007).

92. In Bible interpretation, an "argument from silence" is an argument about which the Bible makes no definitive statement, that presumes facts not in evidence, and that reads into the text the perspective of the writer.

93. A brief biology tutorial: All of life can be classified into a hierarchy of eight levels of increasing specificity: three domains (bacteria, archaea, and eukarya); five kingdoms (monera, protoctisa, fungi, plantae, and animalia); phylum; class; order;

family; genus; and species. If we focus on phylum of animalia, this group includes the sponges, cnidaria (jellyfish and sea anemones), flatworms, rotifera (very tiny wheel-shaped animals), roundworms, segmented worms, mollusks, arthropods (insects, arachnids, and crustaceans), echinodermata (spiny-skinned, like starfish) and chordates (both vertebrates and non-vertebrates). The chordates include fish, amphibians, reptiles, birds, and mammals. And that's enough for this lesson!

94. See Don Patton's website "Bible.ca" at www.bible.ca/tracks/tracks.htm (accessed September 18, 2007).

95. Glen J. Kuban, "The Dinosaur/'Man Track' Controversy 1996-2007," found at http://paleo.cc/paluxy/paluxy.htm (accessed September 18, 2007). Kuban: "Claims of human tracks occurring alongside dinosaur tracks have not stood up to close scientific scrutiny, and in recent years have been largely abandoned even by most creationists."

96. I attended a lecture by Duane Gish back in the 1970s in which he projected on a screen the skeletal structure of a fish and then proceeded to compare the fish with other very different animal skeletons. Whereas in the past it was easier to claim there were no transitional fossils, the claim is much more difficult to maintain as more and more fossils are discovered, scientists will argue.

97. See "Countering Creationism" point #13 on the British Humanist Association's website at www.humanism.org.uk/site/cms/contentviewarticle.asp?article=1499 (accessed September 13, 2007).

98. The position of Howard J. Van Till, emeritus professor of physics and astronomy at Calvin College (Grand Rapids, Michigan) in "The Universe: Accidentally Robust, Intelligently Designed, or Generously Gifted?" on the American Scientific Affiliation website at www.asa3.org/asa/topics/Apologetics/2001VanTill.html (accessed September 19, 2007).

STARLIGHT MONKEYS

99. Ross, p. 92.

MONKEY WRENCHING

100. Phillip E. Johnson, *Defeating Darwinism by Opening Minds* (Downer's Grove, Illinois: InterVarsity Press, 1997), p. 86.

101. Ibid.

102. Michael Denton, *Evolution: A Theory in Crisis* (Adler & Adler, 1986) could definitely be placed within the mainstream Intelligent Design camp. Twelve years later, his *Nature's Destiny: How the Laws of Biology Reveal Purpose in the Universe* (New York: The Free Press, 1998) accepts common descent and goes against "special creation," which makes his latter position difficult to distinguish from Theistic Evolution. See "A Roundtable on *Nature's Destiny*," a discussion by top ID representatives at the Origins and Design website at www.arn.org (accessed May 22, 2007).

103. John Burdon Sanderson Haldane (1892-1964), Scottish-born naturalized Indian geneticist known for his work as a geneticist and application of mathematics

to science; see http://encarta.msn.com/quote_1861506748/God_An_inordinate_ fondness_for_beetles_.html (accessed October 2, 2007).

104. Collins, p. 187.

105. Collins, p. 187.

106. Collins, p. 188.

107. Collins, p. 188.

108. Collins, pp. 188-192.

109. Ayala, p. 26. Ayala's brief history of Intelligent Design arguments before Darwin is very helpful; see pp. 23-26.

CHIMPS, AHOY!

110. Jane Goodall, *Reason for Hope: A Spiritual Journey* (New York: Warner Books, Inc., 1999), p. 80. (In all notations afterward: *Goodall*.)

111. Goodall, p. 67.

112. Goodall, p. 67.

113. This interpretation is in tension with Romans 5:12-21 and with the traditional Christian doctrine of original sin. Theistic evolutionists might make the argument that the problem can be resolved if we take the apostle Paul's words to be metaphorical and not strictly literal and historical.

114. John Haught, *Responses to 101 Questions on God and Evolution* (New York: Paulist Press, 2001) p. 74.

115. Again, reference the BBC website, note number 25 above, for more on Piltdown.

116. The view of Ian G. Barbour in his *Religion and Science: Historical and Contemporary Issues* (San Francisco: HarperSanFrancisco, 1997).

117. See www.gospelway.com/creation/evolution_consequences.php (accessed March 19, 2008).

118. See http://livingtheway.org/SabbathArticles/BelieveInEvolution.html (accessed March 19, 2008).

INHERIT THE SPIN

119. In this chapter I am most indebted to Carol Iannone's "*The Truth about Inherit the Wind* (a play by Jerome Lawrence and Robert E. Lee)," in *First Things* (February 1997), pp. 28-33; see www.firstthings.com/ftissues/ft9702/iannone.html (accessed October 6, 2007).

NO CHIMP LEFT BEHIND

120. See the U.S. Constitution Online website at www.usconstitution.net/const.html (accessed September 26, 2007).

121. If you want to go back further, check out the Idea Center website at www .ideacenter.org/contentmgr/showdetails.php/id/1119 (accessed September 26, 2007).

122. UMKCSL, see www.law.umkc.edu/faculty/projects/ftrials/scopes/tennstat.htm (accessed September 26, 2007).

123. See the Wikipedia summary at http://en.wikipedia.org/wiki/Epperson_v._ Arkansas (accessed September 26, 2007).

124. See the Wikipedia summary at http://en.wikipedia.org/wiki/Lemon_v._ Kurtzman (accessed September 27, 2007).

125. See the Talk Origins summary at www.talkorigins.org/faqs/wright-v-hisd1.html (accessed September 26, 2007).

126. See Mel and Justin Tungate's Mormon apologetics website devoted to summaries of evolution court cases at www.tungate.com/evolution_court_cases.htm (accessed September 27, 2007).

127. See Katherine Ching, "The Teaching of Creation and Evolution in the State of Tennessee" on the Geoscience Research Institute website at www.grisda.org/ origins/01086.htm (accessed September 26, 2007).

128. See Steven Jay Gould's website, http://stephenjaygould.org/ctrl/courtrulings.html (accessed September 26, 2007). (In all notations afterward: *Gould*.)

129. Gould (accessed September 26, 2007).

130. Miller; see the appendix PS section at the end of *Finding Darwin's God*, p. 7.

131. See a summary at the atheism/agnosticism website http://atheism.about.com/ library/decisions/evo/bldec_WebsterNewLenox.htm (accessed September 27, 2007).

132. Gould (accessed September 27, 2007).

133. See the Wikipedia summary at http://en.wikipedia.org/wiki/Freiler_v._ Tangipahoa_Parish_Board_of_Education (accessed September 26, 2007).

134. Molleen Matsumara, "8 Major Court Decisions Against Teaching Creationism as Science" on the National Center for Science Education website at www.ncseweb .org/resources/articles/3747_8_major_court_decisions_agains_2_15_2001.asp (accessed September 26, 2007).

135. See summaries at www.ideacenter.org/contentmgr/showdetails.php/id/1119; and http://en.wikipedia.org/wiki/History_of_the_creation-evolution_controversy (accessed September 27, 2007).

136. Read the Kansas board's decision to go back toward embracing Intelligent Design at the msnbc website, www.msnbc.msn.com/id/9967813/ (accessed February 14, 2008).

137. See the Wikipedia summary at http://en.wikipedia.org/wiki/Teach_the_ Controversy (accessed September 27, 2007).

138. Miller, "PS" section, p. 14; and the Wikipedia summary at http://en.wikipedia. org/wiki/Selman_v._Cobb_County_School_District (accessed September 27, 2007).

139. See "Assistant Superintendent Baksa Developed the Statement [to] Read to Students to Suit the Board and the Teacher[s'] Refusal to Read It," www.talkorigins. org/faqs/dover/pf2.html#p317, paragraphs 245-248 in "Kitzmiller v. Dover Area School District." Complete transcripts of the trial can be found at www.talkorigins. org/faqs/dover/kitzmiller_v_dover.html. They also can be found at: Rob Moll, on *Christianity Today Magazine*'s blog "Pennsylvania Students 'Taught' Intelligent Design," found at www.christianitytoday.com/ct/2005/januaryweb-only/31.0b.html. (Both articles accessed March 19, 2008.)

140. Miller, PS section, pp. 10-11; compare with Collins, pp. 133-141.

141. Miller, PS section, pp. 7-12. See also Wikipedia's summary at http://en. wikipedia.org/wiki/Kitzmiller_v._Dover_Area_School_District (accessed September 27, 2007).

APE OR ANGEL?

142. Ker Than, "Filmmaker Portrays Evolutionists as a "Flock of Dodos,'" on the Live Science website (posted March 3, 2006) at http://livescience.com/health/060303_ flock_dodos.html (accessed October 3, 2007).

143. See *Redeeming Darwin: The Intelligent Design Controversy*, a joint project of Probe Ministries and EvanTell (Richardson, TX: Probe Ministries).

144. John Keats, poet (1795–1821). *Oxford*, p. 290 #27.

A PASSIONATE ENCOUNTER WITH JESUS

JESUS NO EQUAL

by BARRY ST. CLAIR

Get to know
Jesus for who
he really is . . .

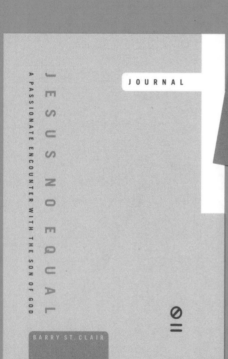

JESUS NO EQUAL JOURNAL

. . . and take a daily
road trip with Jesus
through his life,
death, resurrection,
and second coming.

Standard
PUBLISHING
www.standardpub.com

Find it online at www.standardpub.com,
call 1-800-543-1353,
or visit your local Christian bookstore.